About the cover - A curious observation about a tetrahedron and perception in spacetime is that one cannot view the entire object with our simple stereoscopic vision. At most, we can see three sides, and even then, these sides are distorted. Time is required to view the complete tetrahedron because to see all sides, it must be rotated. The front cover shows a distorted view of three sides of a tetrahedron. The back cover shows the hidden side. The primary colors red, blue, yellow, along with white are used to represent the whole individual. The tetrahedron is shown on a black background to represent the invisible 'dark matter' of the universe in which we all reside.

Four Views of I

Instinct, Intellect, Intuition, and Intention

Stephen Rousseau

BALBOA.
PRESS
A DIVISION OF HAY HOUSE

Balboa Press books may be ordered through booksellers or by contacting:

Balboa Press
A Division of Hay House
1663 Liberty Drive
Bloomington, IN 47403
www.balboapress.com
1 (877) 407-4847

Because of the dynamic nature of the Internet, any web addresses or links contained in this book may have changed since publication and may no longer be valid. The views expressed in this work are solely those of the author and do not necessarily reflect the views of the publisher, and the publisher hereby disclaims any responsibility for them.

The author of this book does not dispense medical advice or prescribe the use of any technique as a form of treatment for physical, emotional, or medical problems without the advice of a physician, either directly or indirectly. The intent of the author is only to offer information of a general nature to help you in your quest for emotional and spiritual well-being. In the event you use any of the information in this book for yourself, which is your constitutional right, the author and the publisher assume no responsibility for your actions.

Any people depicted in stock imagery provided by Getty Images are models, and such images are being used for illustrative purposes only. Certain stock imagery © Getty Images.

Scripture taken from the King James Version of the Bible.

The Holy Bible: International Standard Version. Release 2.0, Build 2015.02.09. Copyright © 1995-2014 by ISV Foundation. ALL RIGHTS RESERVED INTERNATIONALLY. Used by permission of Davidson Press, LLC.

Print information available on the last page.

ISBN: 978-1-9822-0859-2 (sc)
ISBN: 978-1-9822-0857-8 (hc)
ISBN: 978-1-9822-0858-5 (e)

Library of Congress Control Number: 2018908470

Balboa Press rev. date: 08/09/2018

Contents

Inception—Four Words

Allow me to speak of the inception of this book while attempting to help the reader understand a little about who I am. I believe if you know the source, you will have a better understanding of the material.

Escheresque Trinity

When younger, I was a bit obsessed with the Holy Trinity and how it represented me, one made in the image of God. I often sketched triangles and other iconic representations of the Trinity while contemplating. I eventually started repeatedly sketching an Escheresque triangle, which I felt captured the mystery instilled in the Trinity. One day, my worldview was challenged while I was thinking about time and it being the fourth dimension.

I had also been challenged with a Bible verse that implied (or from which I inferred) another level. To me, it spoke of more than three somethings—breadth, length, depth, and height or, as I surmised from this musing, body, mind, soul, and spirit.

Therefore, this book is about four words:

instinct
intellect
intuition
intention

As I live, breathe, read, and experience, I find that the more I know, the more I know I don't know. It is said many of the greatest advancements and discoveries were made by people who were standing on the shoulders of giants. I would like to share the view from atop the giants I have climbed.

The giants I climb take many forms—movies, books, television series, lectures, overheard conversations, seminars, concerts, theater performances, and so on. I am not bound to any genre or theme. I truly enjoy everything, and when I find something I don't like, I try to find out why. I have a rigid facade I wear, but if you get to know me, you will find I have a soft, chewy center.

While listening and discussing, I often skew non sequitur quotes and lyrics.

> Pay no attention to that man behind the curtain.
> —*The Great and Powerful Oz*

You may find some hints of that in this book.

This book is a result of many years' contemplation. After a decade or more, and after I had written most of the book, a friend interjected how similar it was to Elisabeth Kubler-Ross's talk on the four quadrants. She had come to the same conclusion—that everyone is made up of four different aspects: physical, emotional, intellectual, and spiritual. I was not aware she had said anything about this. It is comforting to know there is another giant I didn't even know to climb.

My Intention

Through this book, I intend to share concepts and ideas I have gleaned from my life so far. My sharing should be munched on like salty chips, making you thirsty for more. Keep in mind these are my perceptions and may be skewed by my life choices and experiences.

This book is not intended to be a textbook, and any resemblance to one is unintentional. Don't look for detailed references in what I am sharing. Please view this book as a conversation between me and you. I am simply sharing what I have discovered and learned along the road of life so far.

My advice to you, the reader, is to be serious but don't take it too seriously. Allow the ideas and stories I tell to give you a different perspective. I have learned much and have much more to learn. I always encourage people to question *everything*. There are good people who do bad things and bad people who do good things. It is not as black and white as you'd like. Test all things and hold fast to that which is good. Before we move on to the book, let me tell you a story so you may begin to get to know me.

My View of Authority—Inception

My first lesson in authority occurred during kindergarten at Arlington Elementary in Toledo. (I guess everything I needed to know I really did learn in kindergarten.) Because my birthday is mid-January, I started school a little older than most kids in class. I already knew how to write my name, my address, my phone number, and so on. I was not scared of school—I was excited to be with others and learn. At the time, I went to bed at seven every night and slept well until morning, so the morning naptime in class was alien to me. It was a novelty for the first few days—and of course, I never slept. I had to learn how to look around the room without looking like I was looking. The two teachers were very strict about naptime.

Here is a good spot to insert the fact that my twin sister was in the same classroom, and she suffered the same nap insomnia. As her elder (I was born ten minutes before her), I was held responsible. So I was occasionally punished for not sleeping during naptime—or, more specifically, not allowing others to sleep during naptime (read, my sister). Punishment in this class was separation from the other kids—solitary confinement in the cloakroom.

The cloakroom stretched across the entire back of the room, with a doorway on each end to enter. For a closet, it was a big walk-in one. The heat came in through the cloakroom first and then through a vent into the classroom. (I surmise this was to dry the coats and boots during the school day.) It was nice and warm—and quiet, with the acoustics from the coats hanging on all the walls. It was a nice place to be. My buddies had all been banished to the cloakroom from time to time, and one of them discovered you could climb into the vent duct and look out into the classroom through the grate. Occasionally, we would hide behind a long coat to make it hard for the person sent in to fetch us.

One day, near the end of the school year, the whole class was scheduled to visit a first-grade classroom to see how different it would be—a preorientation of sorts. Because of this anticipated field trip, I was extra antsy during naptime. No surprise, I was sent to the cloakroom. It was a busy time, you know, to indoctrinate the children with rules of walking down the hall into the other class, staying in line, being silent, and so on.

Well, the time had finally come, and one teacher led the children out of the door. The other stayed behind, sweeping the floor, cleaning up clutter, and so on. I was a bit miffed because I was missing out on the field trip. Occasionally, I would peek out the vent to see the teacher sitting quietly in the room. It seemed like forever I was in there. Then, I heard the teacher get up from her chair. Looking out the vent, I watched as she walked to the door, looked around the room one last time before turning off the light and then, she left, slamming the door shut behind her. I waited for a few minutes and then realized they had forgotten about me. I creeped out of the cloakroom, moved across the room, and peeked out the door into an empty hallway. All the classroom doors were closed, and it was very quiet. I wandered down the hallway to the front door of the building and looked out. Nobody was around. So, I walked home.

When I arrived at the house, my mother and her mother (Gran was visiting from England) were sitting on the front porch chatting. Gran saw me first and asked my mother what time it was. My mother looked at me and asked what I was doing home—in a voice that told me I was in trouble. I tried to explain that school was over to no avail. She listened as I told her exactly what happened. She marched me inside and called the school. Then she drove me back to school.

We arrived in the classroom, and I sat in my regular place. The kids were all back and were excitedly telling me how long they had looked for me, assuming I had hidden very well behind one of the coats. One of my buddies even thought to crawl into the vent duct to see if I had climbed up there to hide. Suffice it to say, I received a lecture from both teachers *and* the principal in the short time remaining that day. I then received lectures from my mother and Gran. Then,

I had to wait until "your father gets home" for my last lecture. He told me he understood what had happened. To prove it, his belt stayed on that day.

This was *the* day that built the foundation of my understanding of authority. Authority makes mistakes but rarely, if ever, admits them.

Life, the Universe, et Cetera

Yes, Douglas Adams already told us the answer to the question of life, the universe, and everything is forty-two, but I would like to be a little more explicit. Something is explicit when it is directly stated and leaves no room for uncertainty. It would be wonderful to leave no room for doubt because everything is clearly and directly communicated. Sadly, I won't be doing that here, as there is not enough space in one book to do so. (In fact, there is likely not enough space in all books.) I am afraid the best I can do is be implicit. Something is implicit when it is implied but not directly stated. This leaves a lot of room for interpretation. As you will soon recognize, lately, I have been partial to words that begin with the letter I, so implicit is a better choice anyway.

The Law of One

In my own self-discovery, I have been thinking a lot about the law of one lately. This idea is presented in a series of books channeled through Carla Rueckert, known as *The RA Material*. The basic tenet is everything and everybody is an expression of *the One*. John Lennon said, "I am he as you are he and you are me and we are all together." This view—of what we in the West call God—is intriguing to say the least. Because of this, you will see many concepts in this book some would label "New Age." I ask you to wade through these concepts despite preconceived ideas. I implore you to think about it and always question everything (including your preconceived ideas.)

By the same token, if you are embittered by your past in organized religion, I ask you to take a fresh look at possibilities you may not be aware of. I ask only for an open mind and heart and patience to get to the end of the book. It is only intended to encourage introspection. You always have free will to choose what you believe.

Okay, ready? Let's go!

I-Words

The I's Have It!

Since this book is about four words (*instinct*, *intellect*, *intuition*, and *intention*) that begin with the letter I, I have decided it will contain a lot of words that begin with the same letter. Let's start with the shortest word that begins with i.

It is all about I.

I

The word *I* is the ultimate personal pronoun, referring to oneself (as opposed to one's mother, brother, husband, child, and so on). This English word dates all the way back to before the year 900. Self-identity was and always will be important. The word *I* also refers to your ego.

Could there be a reason those who chose the word chose the ninth letter of the alphabet? In numerology, the number 9 is the symbol of wisdom and initiation. It is the last number before the next harmony. Numerology number 9 has the qualities of all the numbers 1 through 8. Seems to be a wonderful word to begin with.

That said, let's begin with an introduction to the overall premise of this book. (We will use *premise* as a verb, meaning to base an argument, theory, or undertaking on.) This book is a snapshot of my belief system at this point in my life, being what it is.

> When you count, you begin with one, two, three.
> When you read, you begin with A-B-C…
> —*Mary Poppins*

So, let's start at the very beginning too.

Let There Be Light!

A photon has a dual nature of energy and mass. Now, you may say, a photon does *not* have mass! My physics professor told me so! A photon is considered massless because it makes the math easier. There are experiments that prove a photon is a particle. There are other experiments that prove a photon is a wave of energy.

Wave and/or particle, the photon is the initial yin/yang, the foundation of all that is. The photon in *space-time* is the basic building block of what we call reality. The photon phases in and out of existence, the in being *light* and the out being *dark*.

The One perceives *dark* as separate from *light*. *The One* is *all*, so *dark* perceives *the One* and *light*. *Light* perceives *the One* and *dark*. *The One* perceives *light* and *dark*. This is the second dimension—*the plane*.

To perceive *the One*, *light*, and *dark*, *the One* begets another point—*the begotten*. *The begotten* perceives the plane of *the One*, *light*, and *dark*. This is the third dimension—*the object*.

The Begotten

In the beginning was the Word (*the One*). The Word became flesh (*photon*) and dwelt among us (*perception*). Light is the medium of visible life, and time is the expression of life. Moving through time allows the full expression of life.

Take a Look at Yourself

Four Views of I is an introspection into the individual, using words starting with the letter I. We move past the trilogy of body, mind, and soul, adding another dimension: time—the movement of *Spirit*.

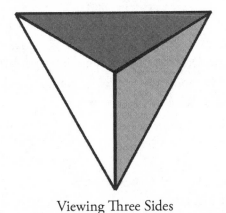

Viewing Three Sides

Body, Mind, Soul, and Spirit

The tetrahedron is the first platonic solid, a shape with four sides. This shape represents the basic building block of our dimension. As energy becomes mass, it takes shape. The simplest form of mass in three dimensions is the tetrahedron. Therefore, in the third dimension, a photon is expressed as a tetrahedron[1]. This is the most basic building block of our perception of our universe. The photon is in this shape. Let there be light!

Everything that is visible is so because of light. Yet visible light is a small portion of the electromagnetic spectrum. Wavicles of existence are included in vibrations far above and below the visible spectrum. X-rays are above; radio and sound waves are below. The holographic existence includes the entire electromagnetic spectrum. All is vibration.

Harmonics are frequencies that are in harmony with each other. For example, an octave above is in harmony with an octave below.

> Harmony and me are pretty good company!
> —Elton John

Dimensions

The smallest unit of 1-D space is a series of points. The point has no mass and no size; it is only location. This is the first manifestation of the *One*.

The smallest representation of 2-D space is a triangle. The triangle is three points joined by three edges. This is the second manifestation of the *One*.

The tetrahedron is the smallest unit of three-dimensional (3-D) space. It is four triangles joined at four corners and contains six edges. This is the third manifestation of the *One*.

Imagine that there is only one photon, and it is the manifestation of the One. Infinite perceptions of this one photon zipping around is

---

[1] https://cosmosmagazine.com/physics/what-shape-is-a-photon

what creates the hologram of all that is. This may sound completely whacky, but consider this story told in a Nobel lecture:

> I received a telephone call one day at the graduate college at Princeton from Professor Wheeler, in which he said, "Feynman, I know why all electrons have the same charge and the same mass." "Why?" "Because, they are all the same electron!"[2]

I am thinking of a cathode ray tube (CRT) and how the entire screen is drawn by a scanning electronic beam one dot at a time. It is done so quickly, it appears to be a complete image. What if this were the same with the entire universe? One electron zipping around so fast it "draws" everything! But I digress.

It's about Time

Now to throw a curve at this. Imagine a curve is infinite points joined together, constantly changing direction. This curve is the fourth dimension we know as time. This curve is combined with the other dimensions to become *space-time*. Everything perceivable is perceived through *space-time*. Time is a curious dimension. Some would say it is not a dimension at all but something outside of space.

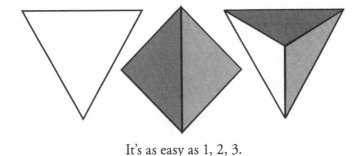

It's as easy as 1, 2, 3.

---

[2] Richard P. Feynman, Nobel Lecture, December 11, 1965

A curious observation about a tetrahedron and perception in *space-time* is that one cannot view the entire object with our simple stereoscopic vision. At most, we can see three sides, and even then, these sides are distorted. Time is required to view the complete tetrahedron because to see all sides, it must be rotated. A series of perceptions are strung together to build a complete perception. Time is required for complete perception.

The Architecture of HuMan—Throne of God

The throne of God is described as surrounded on four sides by cherubim (angels). One has the face of a *lion*. One has the face of an *eagle*. One has the face of an *ox*. And the last has the face of a *man*. Does the God of everything really need to be protected? This seems unlikely. I have heard this arrangement is protection—but not God's. This set of guards is to protect all of creation from the full power and knowledge of God (Revelation 4:6–7).

Here is the question I often brought up in Bible study when the throne of God was taught: If God is surrounded on four cardinal points of the compass, what happens to the other sides—specifically, the bottom and top? I suppose it could be argued the ground at the bottom is secure, but that still leaves us with the top open. Being an air force man, this always bothered me. Or, put another way, an attack could come from the Mole Men (they dig, you know) or the fallen angels (they fly, you know).

We live in a four-dimensional plane. (Yes, physicists say there are more than that, but we can only observe four directly, so we'll go with that.) Four dimensions correspond nicely with the four angels. Let's look again at that most basic Platonic solid, the tetrahedron. It is three dimensions defined. If the four angels were arranged around the power of God in a tetrahedral shape, it would completely encapsulate the power. It is how I came to envision a tetrahedron around the throne of God.

A good visual aid to have handy is a model tetrahedron. We live in a 4-D world. As mentioned, it is generally agreed that the fourth dimension is time. If we want to view our model in 4-D, we must look at it in time. You can perceive the dimension of time by rotating the model.

This model of four planes makes more sense for surrounding the throne completely. Each of the creatures described can have a different plane of existence.

Moving Past the Trinity View

The reason people think of a trinity of parts is because we can only observe a maximum of three of those parts at any one moment. This phenomenon is caused by our three-dimensional life of height, width, and depth. But we now know there is a fourth dimension we can observe, called time or breadth.

Time is a strange dimension in that we cannot fully observe this dimension as we do the other three. We can see back in time but not forward. We can move forward in time but not back. It is a restricted dimension for us.

Let us call this dimension *breadth*. So, the four types that make you up can be observed in height, width, depth, and breadth. Hey, it's biblical!

> May be able to comprehend with all saints what
> is the breadth, and length, and depth, and height;
> And to know the love of Christ, which passeth

knowledge, that ye might be filled with all the
fulness of God.

—Ephesians 3:18–19 (KJV)

These correspond to body, mind, soul, and spirit—the four aspects
of an individual.

Let's Recap

In our *space-time* dimension, we cannot divide these aspects any
further. As with the platonic solid of a tetrahedron, we cannot
make any simpler shape. Because of this, we can use a model of the
tetrahedron to illustrate our limited view.

Here is a page where you can print, cut out, and build your own
model: http://heresyman.com/build-your-own-tetrahedron-model
(right click on the picture, and paste it into a document; then you
can print it, cut it, fold it, and glue it).

The only way to view all four sides of a tetrahedron is to rotate the
object. Time is required to observe all that you are. So, hold the
model in your hand, and try to look at all four sides. You can't do it.
The only way to see all four sides is to rotate the tetrahedron. Time
allows you to do this.

Life goes on! Be an active part! Life is for living!

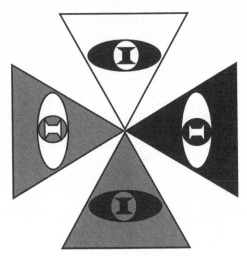

Four Triangles, Four I's

Four I's

The individual is composed of four aspects: body, mind, soul, and spirit. Envision each triangle face of a tetrahedron as representing each aspect. I chose to assign a name to each of the triangle faces—instinct, intellect, intuition, and intention. I chose these words because they all begin with I. (See what I did there?) Not only that, they are descriptive of each aspect. I posit these are descriptive of the four aspects of every human being. These aspects are what make up your identity. We all have all four, but the ratio between the four aspects make each of us unique. In a perfect world, all tetrahedrons would be made up of four identical equilateral triangles, like the model. Each of us may have different sizes and shapes of triangles making up our throne.

Womb to Tomb

Life on this plane of existence is brief. Most live less than one hundred years, although many today will pass that. Some advances may even bring this to a much higher number of years, but even at a thousand years, what is that compared to eternity?

Life Is a Dash!

Our entire life is summed up in that little dash between the birth date and the date of death on the tombstone. Each of us arrived separately. Each of us are a separate manifestation of I Am. Whether this manifestation happened at conception or at the beginning of time is not clear. I am here. No matter where I go, there I am. Each of us departs separately.

Inner-Space

Be an introvert. By this, I mean, get your strength from within. Don't expect others to change you—you are the only person who can change you. Are you in service to self or service to others? I hope you know.

You cannot effectively serve others unless your self *is* centered. How do you get your self-centered without becoming self-centered? Is there really a difference?

It is a matter of focus: introversion verses extroversion. Even these words are misunderstood by most. It is imperative that we use words with the same understanding of their definitions. So, for me, an introvert is someone who gains strength from within him- or herself. An extrovert is someone who gains strength from outside of him- or herself.

An introvert has a centered self, with everything going toward others. An extrovert is self-centered, drawing everything toward him- or herself.

Choose to Center Yourself

Are you *self-centered*, or is your self *centered*?

When you are self-centered, you put yourself at the center of the universe. You draw energy from outside in. Everything revolves around you. You are demanding.

When you have a centered self, you draw the power from within and you revolve around everything. You are in demand.

Center of the Universe

The center of the universe is at the center of I. Think about this: everything else in the universe is outside of you. That puts you right in the center of it all!

Pyramid (Fire in the Middle)

The tetrahedron is a pyramid shape. I have heard the word *pyramid* means a "pyre in the middle." If so, it means the fire of God burns in each of us. Shine on!

Information

Know thyself! As you visualize the whole you, rotate the view and look at every angle. It takes time; live in the now, continuously in motion. Information means forming within. You will discover two physical aspects are embodied in body and mind, and two metaphysical aspects are embodied in soul and spirit. Work with these pairs together at first, and then pair up a physical aspect with a metaphysical aspect, and work with it as a pair. Try *body/mind* and *soul/spirit* at first. Then switch to *body/soul* and *mind/spirit*. Try every combination! Move to a triad of three, and remember, you can only see three sides of the tetrahedron at a time—one, two, or three aspects at a time—while stuck in our 3-D plane. Take time. It's always there, slipping into the future!

Only You!

One is the loneliest number you will ever know. One is all you are. Realize you are a facet of *the One* who overcame loneliness by creating everything.

Do what thou wilt! Free will is yours to exercise or relinquish. If you relinquish your will to another, you always have the choice to take it back. No matter, you are fully responsible either way. Choose wisely!

Responsibility—it is always there, and giving it away does not free you of it. Since you are ultimately responsible for every aspect of your life, keep control of it—all four aspects!

Transformation—time is the dimension of transformation. Don't wait for transformation to find you. Go forth and become.

Surely Temple—Pyramid

The New Testament teaches that each of us is the temple of God. We surely are, because we have infinity inside of us. Look within to find the truth.

Reiteration

Repetition is the key to retention.

In the beginning was the Word (*the One*). The Word became flesh (*photon*) and dwelt among us (*perception*).

Dimensionality

Zero-dimensional space is a point. The point has no mass and no size; it is only location. It is nothing. From this nothing comes everything—ex nihilo.

First Dimension

The smallest unit of 1-D space is a line between two points. This is the first manifestation of the One—the begetting.

Second Dimension

The smallest representation of 2-D space is a triangle. The triangle is three points joined by three edges. There is stability in the triangle. This trinity is the second manifestation of the One.

Third Dimension

The tetrahedron is the smallest unit of 3-D space. It is four triangles joined at four corners and six edges. This is the third manifestation of the One. The tetrahedron is the basic building block and is the first Platonic solid. It is built with locations joined by straight lines.

Fourth Dimension

Now to throw a curve at this. A curve is infinite points joined together, constantly changing direction. I propose this curve is the fourth dimension we know as time. This curve is combined with the other dimensions to become *space-time*. Everything perceived is perceived through *space-time*. Time is a curious dimension. Some would say it is not a dimension at all but something outside of space.

The shape of the photon is tetrahedral. The photon in *space-time* is the basic building block of what we call reality.

Other Dimensions

Incredibly, there are other dimensions, but we cannot perceive them except by inference.

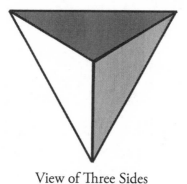

View of Three Sides

Perception in 4-D Space

A curious observation about a tetrahedron and perception in *space-time* is that we cannot view the entire object with our stereoscopic vision. At most, we can see three sides, but these sides are distorted. It takes time to view the complete tetrahedron because it must be rotated. A series of perceptions are strung together to build a complete perception. Time is required for complete perception.

I used to think time was an anomaly. But I now believe it is a tool for perception. Time appears to be a half dimension to provide increased perception, which works toward completion. A continuous creation is what time-space is.

Independent

Independence Day

Who do you think you are? What you think is, is. If you think you are a loser, you are. If you think you are a winner, you are. An individual is indivisible. Individuality is your essence. It is who you are—all that you are. Know yourself!

Individual

Change is growth. Curve is change. Everyone is different—that's the point! Everyone must change to grow. Change takes time.

I am he as you are he as you are me and we are all together!
–The Beatles

Embrace diversity!

What Am I? Who Am I? Where Am I? Why Am I?

What am I? Who am I? Where am I? Why am I? To me, these four questions relate to the four aspects of I. The question "What am I?" is answered in instinct, or the body. "Who am I?" is answered in intelligence, or the mind. "Where am I?" is answered in intuition, or the soul. "Why am I?" is answered in intention, or the spirit.

Here are a couple of *I* words to keep in mind:

Independent

Independent means not dependent on another. "I am he as you are he as you are I and we are all together!" Depending on self is depending on the Source. Be all that you can be!

Iceberg

We all know that most of an iceberg is below the surface. Most of I is below the surface too. If you want to know who you are, you've got to look under the surface.

Four Dimensions

We exist in four dimensions. Superstring theory proposes ten dimensions, four of which are knowable; the rest are curled up into regions unknowable to us[3]. For our purposes, I will focus on the four we can know.

Four or Three-and-a-Half?

As energy becomes mass, it takes shape. The simplest form of three-dimensional (3-D) mass is the tetrahedron. Therefore, in the third dimension, a photon is expressed as a tetrahedron. This is the most basic building block of our perception of our universe.

There is only one photon, which is the manifestation of the One. Infinite perceptions of this One photon create the hologram of all that is. Time is the fourth dimension. Apparently, all we perceive is 4-D space-time (well, some would say 3.5-D).

---

[3] https://www.universetoday.com/48619/a-universe-of-10-dimensions/

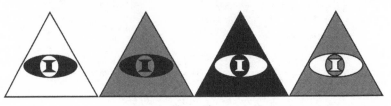

Four I's

Four I's—Instinct, Intellect, Intuition, Intention—*Make You Individual*

Every human is made of these four aspects: body, mind, soul, and spirit. Move past the triune view of yourself, and understand the tetragrammaton, the four Hebrew letters that represent the name of God. It is the fourth aspect that allows the full motion picture. The 2-D view of 3-D is flat and incomplete. Put yourself in motion to have a 3-D view of 4-D. (At this point, it's good to have a model tetrahedron handy.)

Introducing Introspection

Take your model tetrahedron, hold it, and look at it. You only have two eyes. Even with stereoscopic vision, you cannot see the whole tetrahedron at once. There is always at least one side missing. (Perhaps a person with an activated third eye could see the whole.)

Rotate the tetrahedron. It is only with motion in time that you will gain knowledge of the whole. It takes time (deep thought there).

Tetrahedron—Photon

Before the beginning, the One was nothing and nowhere, self-aware and lonely. The One is Creator and so creates light. The basic unit of light is a photon. A photon has a dual nature as energy and mass, wave and particle. The term *wavicle* is often used to describe it.

Heresyman: Origin Story

A few years back, I took on the moniker "Heresyman." Here is the *Reader's Digest* version of how that happened.

Several years ago, the church I had been attending in San Clemente dissolved and blended into another local church. I was on the elder board at the time and actively worked with the team to ensure the blending went as smoothly as possible. Without going into details, I decided at that time that the new blended church would not be a great fit for me.

So, I started attending another, well-established church that was growing and quite popular in the area. For a month or two, I plugged in, attended the Sunday services, and tried to get to know people. One Sunday, the church was having a meeting after the last service to make some corporate decisions or some such, and wanting to be involved, I stayed after to attend. To my surprise, I was turned away at the door because I was not a "member." I apologized for being ignorant and asked how one became a member. I discovered that I must attend membership classes. So, I signed up and sat through the explanation of how the church is governed and which verses of the Bible are the basis.

After three or four weeks of training, we had our final exam. It was a series of statements, and you had to mark off whether or not you agreed with them. One of the statements basically said that if you disagreed with the pastor, you would keep it to yourself. Another said that you would not teach anything to others that didn't agree with the pastor, even outside church activities on your own time. Being me, of course, I marked the "do not agree" boxes. Needless to say, I was called to meet with the pastor.

To make a long story short, I refused to change my answers on principle. He suggested if I didn't like the way he ran his church, I should start my own. He told me I was welcome to continue as an attender, but I was not welcome to be a member. I intended to start going to the services wearing a scarlet letter A. That way, if I were asked what the A was for, I could say I was branded an "attender." But out of respect for my very embarrassed wife, I agreed to find another church.

After my inquisition (hey, another *I* word), I decided to look up the definition of heresy. The following is extracted from dictionary.com:

> heretic
>
> her-i-tik
>
> noun
>
> A professed believer who maintains religious opinions contrary to those accepted by his or her church or rejects doctrines prescribed by that church. Roman Catholic Church: a baptized Roman Catholic who willfully and persistently rejects any article of faith. Anyone who does not conform to an established attitude, doctrine, or principle.

Once I had discovered heresy had nothing to do with God but everything to do with organized religion, I started referring to myself as Heresyman.

Who Am I? Who Are You?

"I think; therefore, I am" (*cogito ergo sum*—for those who prefer the Latin). I am conscious, but the question is still "Who am I?"

When Moses asked God His name, so he could tell the people who sent him, God said, "Tell them that I Am sent you" (or *I will be who I will be* or *I am the one who is*).

> God replied to Moses, "I AM WHO I AM," and then said, "Tell the Israelis: 'I AM sent me to you.'"
> —Exodus 3:14 (ISV)

So, that tells us who He is—but what about me? You? Everyone?

Command: Whoami

Back in the day, before cool, graphical user interfaces (GUIs) were integrated into operating systems (OSs), it was hard to tell who was logged into a terminal. A bit of code was burned into the firmware of the computer so when the command *whoami* was entered, the computer would provide data to let you know the name of the user the computer was responding to.

Oh, if only it were that easy in real life. "Who am I?" may never be answered in a lifetime. But if there is an equivalent to *whoami* in our personal lives, I would put my money on accessing it through meditation.

Of the four words—*instinct, intellect, intuition,* and *intention,* I consider the first two words physical attributes and the other two metaphysical (spiritual). Yes, I know we can argue about semantics, but as the author, I get to choose the meaning. I have the right to write as I see fit. Explaining the terms is part of the communication process. Thank you for your understanding.

But that all should become clear later—let's move on and look at the four views of *I.*

Investigate—Physics

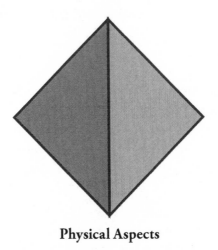

Physical Aspects

As we move around the tetrahedron, we find two sides that represent the physical: the body and mind. These are instinct and intellect, respectively. They are represented in physics.

Physics is the natural science that studies matter and its motion and behavior through space and time, as well as the related entities of energy and force.

For the purposes of this book, we will simply call physics and the physical the *physical aspects*. Extracted from dictionary.com are the following definitions:

phys·ics

fiziks

noun: physics

The branch of science concerned with the nature and properties of matter and energy. The subject matter of physics, distinguished from that of chemistry and biology, includes mechanics, heat, light and other radiation, sound, electricity, magnetism, and the structure of atoms. The physical properties and phenomena of something.

phys·i·cal

fizik(ə)l

adjective: physical

Relating to the body as opposed to the mind. Involving bodily contact or activity. Relating to things perceived through the senses as opposed to the mind; tangible or concrete.

Many years ago, I came across a book titled *You Are What You Read* in a Christian bookstore. I flipped it over to the back cover to glimpse what it was about. As I suspected, the author seemed to imply that a good Christian restricts reading to Christian books, or some such. At least that is what the synopsis on the back led me to believe. I put the book down, not because I disagreed with the title but because I disagreed with the conclusion.

This bookstore event came back to mind today while I was thinking about the power of thought. I did a quick search to see if I could find the book on Amazon but couldn't. I don't remember the author's name, and I assume it is out of print. No matter, I probably still wouldn't purchase it. Although if an inexpensive Kindle version were available ...

I am completely against banning books. Burning books is anathema to me. *Fahrenheit 451* comes to mind. The burning of the library at Alexandria is a tragedy of *epic* proportions. Don't get me started.

Anyway, I have always said all books should be read. Warnings about the content may be placed on the wrapper, like the opaque covering of adult magazines. Book censorship is not as big a problem today, however. Reading is too slow for the modern age. Books are passé.

The last few years of reading books by David Wilcock and others speaking of secret space programs made me wonder about the possibility that I was part of the secret space program. (Of course, I had my mind wiped when my enlistment ended; that's why I can't remember it.) This is not the first time I thought something like this may have happened. I also had thoughts along these lines when I read Peter Moon's Montauk books. Yes, I read many strange books—and I admit, they have influenced me. I did my daily Bible study for many years. I do not regret any of it. Laissez-faire is the attitude I extend to reading. Read a wide variety of things. If you have a book that teaches one thing, and there are books refuting it, read them too!

Let me insert my analogy of lottery scratch-offs. The one big winning ticket can only be in one location, so if you never go to that liquor store that has that particular ticket, you will *never* win the big prize. If you want to find that ticket, increase your odds by buying at multiple locations.

Movies, television, streaming, and narrations are bumping books from the scene. News flash: Amazon is not what shut down the big bookstores; technology did. Verbal storytelling was replaced by books when the general population became literate. Books have been replaced by television and movies now the general population has become lazy.

No matter if it is stories around the campfire, the latest binge on Netflix, the latest blockbuster movie, or the latest blog, book, or cereal box you've read, memes are injected.

I find the word *investigate* fits the physical aspects best because they are tangible. We simply are the way we are, and it is up to us to decide what to do with what we are. Extracted from dictionary.com is the following definition:

in·ves·ti·gate

in'vestə‚gāt

verb

Carry out a systematic or formal inquiry to discover and examine the facts of (an incident, allegation, etc.) so as to establish the truth.

Since the body is the visible aspect of our identity, it behooves us to investigate how it works and maintain it well. In truth, the dividing line between physical and spiritual is very fuzzy. Investigation of the whole I begins with instinct.

Instinct

To keep things as clear as possible, I believe it best to define words as I, the author, use them. This chapter is to help do just that. I will endeavor to explain how I am using a word as I go throughout this book.

So, what do I mean by the word *instinct*? Let's start with a dictionary definition (from dictionary.com):

> in·stinct
>
> ˈin-ˌstiŋ(k)t
>
> noun
>
> Natural or inherent aptitude, impulse, or capacity. A largely inheritable and unalterable tendency of an organism to make a complex and specific response to environmental stimuli without involving reason. Behavior that is mediated by reactions below the conscious level.

Examples of *instinct* include the following:

- Our first *instinct* was to run.
- Cats possess a natural hunting *instinct*.
- Seeing the baby aroused all her maternal *instincts*.

- He has been guided throughout his career by his political *instincts*.
- Mere *instinct* alerted her to the danger.
- He knew *by instinct* what not to say.
- She seemed to know *by instinct* that something was wrong.
- He has a strong survival *instinct*.
- She is an athlete with good *instincts*.

I consider instinct to be a physical attribute of who I am.

So many things are hardwired into our bodies, and we do them without thinking. The first thing you did when you were born was to start breathing. Breathing is an instinct. Your heartbeat is an instinct and was going long before you were born. Eating is another automatic instinct. Right from the start, you knew how to suck the nourishment from your mother. In a computer analogy, we would call this the *firmware*.

Migration

Migration is an instinct in many animals and insects. One of my favorite interactions with a migration happens in Maui, Hawaii. The gray whales migrate to the warm waters of Hawaii during the winter months. I don't blame them. Hawaii is my go-to vacation destination too. Maui also happens to be the nursery for the gray whales. They spend the winter months producing new pod members. So, there is a lot of excitement and motion in the water during this time. There is plenty of food for the mothers to produce milk for the new babies. When the babies are born, they instinctively know to breathe when their blowhole breaks the surface of the water. Their mothers may need to nudge them to the surface, but they don't open that blowhole until it is in the air. If you are there at the correct time of year, you can sit on the lanai of your hotel room and watch the bull whales breach. It is a very exciting and relaxing way to spend a few hours.

Oh, the reason I brought up the whales is the most wonderful experience I had was swimming off the shore. As soon as my ears were in the water, I could hear whale song. Whale song was something I had heard from recordings, but to put my ear underwater and hear the whales talking real time was magical. I highly recommend listening if you are ever in Maui at the correct time of year. If you are good at floating on your back, just lie back and listen. You can begin to discern by the sounds they make when feeding time is, when there is danger, or when they are just playing.

I remember as a young boy watching the Canada geese fly over Toledo on their way south. I was (still am) fascinated by the way they fly in a V-shape. That is something they do instinctively. How do they know how to conserve energy by drafting the goose in front? How does the strongest goose get selected to fly up front? How do they know which way to go? When to go? When to come back?

I Just Know

Come to think of it, how do you know to keep your mouth and nose shut when underwater? How do you know how to swim up to the surface? We aren't whales, so how did we get this instinct? The point is, like a homing pigeon, we just know.

Double Helix

Deoxyribonucleic acid, or DNA, is a self-replicating material present in nearly all living organisms as the main constituent of chromosomes. It is the carrier of genetic information. DNA is a double helix (RNA is a single helix). Both have sets of nucleotides that contain genetic information. DNA is a molecule that contains the instructions an organism needs to develop, live, and reproduce.

Is instinct hardwired into our DNA? DNA is an incredible code that is just now starting to be decoded. DNA is binary, self-correcting, and self-replicating. I would like to point out that this binary code is made up of four components. Hey, what if these represent the four I's? Also, there is evidence that DNA attracts photons. Yes, you read that correctly. DNA attracts photons. As it sits there, any loose photon floating by is attracted to and rests in the double helix. When you move the DNA away, the photons will stay in place, showing right where the DNA molecule was resting. I don't know about you, but to me, this is a mind-blowing thought.

Perhaps DNA is a physical address of who and what you are. It is completely unique to you. There are no two people with the same DNA—ever. Even a clone will have a small, albeit very hard to discern, difference. I am a twin. Siblings have many commonalities in their DNA. The same is true with cousins, aunts, and uncles; they all have familial DNA. Science has brought us to the point where we can spit in a tube, send it in, and within a few weeks receive a chart of where our ancestors came from. (So, has anyone tested the blood from the Shroud of Turin? What is Jesus's blood type? What was his familial DNA like? I mean, wasn't his dad the Holy Spirit?)

There is so much information available in DNA, no wonder it is said to be the tree of life.

Two Trees

That reminds me, in the Garden of Eden, two trees are specifically named. One was the Tree of the Knowledge of Good and Evil. This is the tree Adam and Eve were forbidden to eat from. The other was the Tree of Life. Notice that this tree was *not* forbidden. I suggest that these two trees represent the two angels on the top of the Ark of the Covenant. They represent the physical and metaphysical aspects that make up humankind. I suspect the tree of life is guarded because we are not meant to live forever physically. We are meant to live forever spiritually; in fact, we cannot do anything else. What exactly is that Tree of the Knowledge of Good and Evil? It is transcendental, I am sure. These two trees still exist in the Garden of Eden, wherever that is now. It is guarded by two angels with flaming swords. (Hey, perhaps that is where the other two angels from God's throne went. You know, the two not on the Ark of the Covenant.)

Another thing about DNA—scientists had assumed much of the code was just "garbage" or "junk DNA" left over from failed evolutionary experiments. But just because the section of DNA is dormant doesn't mean that it is not there for a reason. They are beginning to realize that the dormant DNA can be activated to perform the tasks it was designed for.

Immortality

Immortality, now *that* is an I-word worth looking into. Telomeres are the little bits of code at the end of the chromosomes. Many people liken telomeres to the end of a shoelace. The end of the shoelace has a bit of plastic wrapped around it to keep it from fraying. It is said telomeres perform the same function, keeping the chromosomes from unraveling. Each time DNA is duplicated, a little bit of the telomeres is lost. Eventually, the telomeres become ineffective and the DNA starts to unravel. It is said this is the main cause of aging— we lose more and more of the code for rebuilding. If we can keep the telomeres from shrinking, we can stop aging. As a matter of fact, the body does produce adult stem cells that have complete DNA. If the damaged cell is removed and replaced with a stem cell, aging can be reversed. By making sure the telomeres are never shortened and all the damaged cells are replaced, we can live forever.

Physically, our body continues reproducing and replacing cells moment by moment, hour by hour, day by day—never stopping.

How often do you stop and think about each of these cells or even a group of these cells—likely, *never*. But if those cells go bad and turn cancerous, I bet you will think about them! The body just keeps moving forward with the instruction set it has available. If the instruction set gets corrupted, then the harmony is disrupted. Therefore, I consider the physical body to be under the control of the instinct aspect of human life.

Cellular biology has grown leaps and bounds since I studied it in school. Back then, we only had a few labels to remember on a cell. We only needed to remember a few components. But so much more has been discovered about the parts of a cell. It is less of a mystery than ever before. It is a field all its own now. The complication of the little bits inside a cell is extraordinary. No wonder DNA must contain so much data. Each living cell has its own copy of DNA. DNA is a blockchain—the ultimate blockchain. You have your own cryptocurrency keeping you running. Gene therapy is possible. That is mind-blowing!

Embrace Change

You can actually change your DNA. In fact, DNA is altered by inputs you receive. Chemicals can change your DNA—activating new sections, cutting in new sections. Once the blockchain is altered, the rest of the copies change to comply with the new set of instructions. It is a hard reset—like turning your computer off and on again. If you do this incorrectly, some vital information may be lost. By the same token, it seems possible to put aside some stem cells in cryostasis for therapy if this should happen. We are at an incredible time in history. Technology is a wondrous tool—or are we playing with fire? How many civilizations in the past have come to this point and burned the world by accident? How many cycles of learning has humankind been through? What really happened in Atlantis? But that is a subject for another book.

Belief is a big deal for your instinct. Oh, and instinct can be instilled. You can learn to react instinctively. A person can overcome a fear of heights, for example, by putting faith in safety equipment. Why do some people have a fear of heights and others don't? Perhaps it has to do with a traumatic fall earlier in life (or in an earlier life). The glass bridges are a good place to overcome fear. One of the first things a person must learn is not to look down! There is a video on the interwebs that shows a person walking out on a glass-bottom bridge. What the person doesn't know is that the glass is also an LCD display. When the person steps on a certain part of the bridge, the LCD will come on showing the glass shatter right where he or she just stepped. If the person panics or moves more, the glass continues to look as if it is shattering completely. It is rather comical to see the person jump and try to grab onto the railing to keep from plummeting into the abyss.

Physical Exercise

Physical exercise is something that used to be purely instinctive. Running from predators, chasing after prey, reproducing, and so on were all plenty of exercise. Paleolithic humans were very fit indeed, and it is no wonder so many people try to replicate the diet of these prehistoric humans. Of course, the life span of Paleolithic humans is estimated to have been around thirty-five years. It wasn't the years; it was the mileage. There is much to be said about diet and exercise for a long life. Fasting is another form of longevity extension therapy. This is going against instinct. The body needs fuel to function. Cutting off that fuel supply is detrimental. The body was designed, or evolved, or whatever, to deal with temporary fuel shortages. For hunter/gatherers, this was a common occurrence. See, things didn't always grow and ripen, and sometimes the prey was too fast. It was not uncommon to go a week or two without feeding. But, the hungrier people got, the more desperate they became. During these times of fasting, the body would utilize fats it had stored up. This was also a good time to get rid of the old cells that weren't productive any longer—survival of the fittest in the body. It is thought that fasting kicks in ketosis and other processes that cleanse the entire system of undesirables—running the company lean and mean, so to speak. It uses up all the fat reserves and streamlines processes to conserve energy. The problem with ketosis is any food input the body does receive is immediately sent to reserves, which makes sense because that is where all the energy is being derived. In our modern age, putting the body in ketosis while still supplying the body with sugars and other carbohydrates adds weight to the body.

Nutrition

This brings up a pet peeve of mine, artificial sweeteners. Here is what happens when you give your body artificial sweeteners. The taste buds all report that the body is receiving sugars and carbs, and the brain logs it in as so. The only problem is the cells that need the sugars to survive are shortchanged. The checks from headquarters bounce, and they are left holding the bag. Of course, they scream they need more sugars, and the riots begin. Cravings go off the charts. Eating anything that is artificially sweetened is counterproductive to any weight-loss regimen. Here is a good analogy. Artificial sweeteners are like flooding the market with counterfeit money. Trust in the money is quickly lost. You are better off eating foods with good, natural sugars than diet food. Oh, that brings up another problem, highly processed sugars. Using highly processed sugars in foods is like hyperinflation in the economy. Soon, you have people taking wheelbarrows full of paper money just to get the bread they need to live. Oh, and the paper money is giving your cells paper cuts and infection. It is a bad thing. Soon the banks all close their doors, and depression hits. Insulin does nothing, so it just stops being injected into the system. There is no reason; the regulation of the money system is worthless. Bank Pancreas must lock its doors. "Hey, buddy, can you spare a dime for a fellow American down on his luck?" The soup kitchen is overworked, and society breaks down, metaphorically speaking.

Immigration

So, in summary, physically, you are made up of billions of individual cells all working together in unison. Here is an interesting fact: the biome inside your gut has more macrobiotics (microscopic entities that are *not* you) than you have cells in your body. These are the alien workers who keep your economy going. Sure, you can build a wall and send in the police force of antibiotics to remove them, but you do so to your own detriment. We need that symbiosis to live! Stop killing the immigrants, and live in peace with them.

Never Mind

A person can survive on instinct alone but only at the basest of levels. Doing so will not be conducive to a good community. If you don't mind your mind, you may regret it.

Intellect

Intellect is the second I-word on my list. It is also the second physical aspect in my understanding. Intellect is all about what happens in the brain at a conscious level.

Let's begin again with a dictionary definition (from dictionary.com):

> in·tel·lect
>
> ˈin-tə-ˌlekt
>
> noun
>
> The power of knowing as distinguished from the power to feel and to will: the capacity for knowledge. The capacity for rational or intelligent thought, especially when highly developed. A person with great intellectual powers.

Examples of *intellect* include the following:

- She is a woman of superior *intellect*.
- She has a sharp *intellect*.
- We were required to read a book every week in order to develop our *intellects*.
- It is music that appeals to the *intellect* while still satisfying the emotions.

For the purposes of this book, I will use the word *mind* synonymously with the word *brain*, as a starting point. An incredible amount of information storage space is available in the brain. We now have tools (albeit very expensive ones) that can map the electronic impulses going on in a brain in real time. The brain is an incredible computing/data storage/problem-solving electrochemical machine. The brain has different discernable parts, which have different functions. Three of our senses are wired directly into this lump of gray matter, apparently to shorten the distance in time from when the signal occurs to when it registers in the brain. These three senses are eyesight, hearing, and smell. Eyesight and hearing are receiving frequency signals in the electromagnetic spectrum. Smell is converting chemical signals into electronic signals. I suppose we have two spectrum analyzers and one electrochemical converter. Along with these senses, we have taste and touch. Now that I think about it, taste is wired very close to the brain also. It is another electrochemical converter and also includes temperature sensors and tactile receptors of touch. Touch has receptors all over the body with concentrations in special places like the fingertips and feet. Again, all these receptors feed data directly to the brain for processing.

Eyesight is split into two cameras that have a very interesting interface with the brain. While most of the body is split into two and controlled by the opposite hemisphere of the brain, the eyes are wired and controlled by both sides simultaneously. Perhaps this direct connection is why we say, "Seeing is believing." It may also be wired this way simply for depth perception in a 3-D world. The images are received moment by moment, and the brain combines the moments into a streaming video of the world in real-time 3-D. Photons are collected on the retina and converted into signals very close to the input of the brain. Even though the speed of light is the fastest thing in the universe, there is still a bit of a delay from when the light strikes the retina and the converted signal reaches the brain. This explains the design (or fortuitous desultory accident of evolution) of placing the eyes as close as possible to the brain. When things are happening fast and furious, the brain must be able to respond.

Here is an interesting "fact" I remember learning in school. Once you've reached the age of puberty, all the brain cells you have left are permanent. They will never be replaced. They are all you get and all you will ever get, so be careful. Perhaps this false conclusion was reached because we tend to kill so many brain cells with alcohol as soon as we can drink (some sooner). There is a difference between killing off the brain cells faster than they can be replaced and the brain cells dying of old age. More recent studies have proven that brain cells do, in fact, get replaced. Not that we need them—I mean, the jellyfish has no brain to replace, yet it contains a chemical we can extract and use on ourselves to encourage brain cell replacement. (Yes, I am sarcastically making fun of a supplement available on the market.)

Oh, let's talk about Homebody Security. The amygdala is a portion of the brain known as the reptile brain because it acts without conscious knowledge when a decision of fight or flight is needed. Your body has so much data streaming into it, your conscious mind in the frontal lobe cannot keep track of it all. Picture a control center like at NASA used in the moon landings. There are dozens of small monitors along the rows of desk stations where Team Amygdala watches the happenings of the inputs. Each station is capable of tuning in to many data streams, and some continually flip through, looking for something important. Some of these monitors are fixed on a particular data stream that is important to the mission, or mission critical. There is a lot of activity going on down on the floor. In front of them all is a large projected screen that can display up to six of the monitors from the floor. Or it can show four, two, or one image. Again, it all depends on the import of the data and what is critical for the frontal lobe to concentrate on. Our frontal lobe is a serial processor, meaning it can only focus on one thing at a time. Even if there are six views playing at the same time, only one can be the focus. The reason you want to have six views is so you can quickly switch focus between them. It is still done one at a time. The personnel down on the floor are each processing their own screen, so in this case, they are simulating parallel processing.

The Brain

Let's look at how the brain is constructed. For a lump of gray matter, it sure has a lot to do. It is divided into sections, lobes, and specific bits, which all interact in a way requiring all the parts. If a section is damaged, the body will make do with what is left, often providing the same function in a different area of the brain. The brain is many parts yet an integrated whole. (That's a nice I-word.)

Cerebral Cortex

The cerebral cortex is the outermost layer of the cerebral hemisphere. It is composed of gray matter. Cortices are asymmetrical. Both hemispheres analyze sensory data, perform memory functions, learn new information, form thoughts, and make decisions. The cerebral cortex controls your thinking, voluntary movements, language, reasoning, and perception. In higher mammals, the cortex looks like it has lots of wrinkles, grooves, and bumps.

Cerebrum

This is the largest brain structure in humans and accounts for about two-thirds of the brain's mass. It is divided into two sides—the left and right hemispheres—which are separated by a deep groove down the center from the back of the brain to the forehead. These two halves are connected by long neuron branches called the corpus callosum, which is relatively larger in women's brains than in men's. The cerebrum is positioned over and around most other brain structures, and its four lobes are specialized by function but are richly connected. The outer three millimeters of gray matter form the cerebral cortex, which consists of closely packed neurons that control most of our body functions, including the mysterious state of consciousness, the senses, the body's motor skills, reasoning, and language.

Left Hemisphere

The left hemisphere does sequential analysis—systematic, logical interpretation of information. It is also responsible for interpretation and the production of symbolic information—language, mathematics, abstraction, and reasoning. Memory is stored in a language format.

Corpus Callosum

The corpus callosum facilitates communication between the two hemispheres.

Right Hemisphere

The right hemisphere is responsible for holistic functioning—processing multisensory input simultaneously to provide a holistic picture of one's environment—and visual spatial skills. Holistic functions, such as dancing and gymnastics, are coordinated by the right hemisphere. Memory is stored in auditory, visual, and spatial modalities.

Midbrain

This section controls your breathing and reflexes, like your swallowing reflex. It includes the thalamus, hippocampus, and amygdala. Every living thing must have a midbrain.

Thalamus

Located at the top of the brain stem, the thalamus relays messages between lower brain centers and the cerebral cortex, acting as a two-way relay station, sorting, processing, and directing signals from the spinal cord and midbrain structures up to the cerebrum. It controls your sensory and motor integration. The thalamus receives sensory information and relays it to the cerebral cortex. The cerebral cortex also sends information to the thalamus, which then transmits this information to other parts of the brain and the brain stem.

Amygdala

Lying deep in the neural centers in the limbic system linked to emotion, this powerful structure, the size and shape of an almond, is constantly alert to the needs of basic survival, including sex and emotional reactions, such as anger and fear. Consequently, it inspires aversive cues, such as sweaty palms, and has recently been associated with a range of mental conditions, including depression and even autism. It is larger in male brains and is often enlarged in the brains of sociopaths, and it shrinks in the elderly. The amygdalae (there are two of them) control your emotions, such as regulating when you're happy or mad. Your amygdala is very important. Without it, you could win the lottery and feel nothing. You wouldn't be happy.

Pons

The pons is part of the metencephalon in the hindbrain. It is involved in motor control and sensory analysis—for example, information from the ear first enters the brain in the pons. It has parts that are important for the level of consciousness and for sleep, as it relays information between the cerebrum and the cerebellum, controls arousal, and regulates respiration. Some structures within the pons are linked to the cerebellum and thus are involved in movement and posture.

Medulla Oblongata

This structure is the caudal-most part of the brain stem, between the pons and spinal cord. It is responsible for maintaining vital body functions, such as heartbeat and breathing.

Spinal Cord

The spinal cord is the pathway for neural fibers traveling to and from the brain; it controls simple reflexes.

Brain Stem

The brain stem is the part of the brain that connects to the spinal cord. The brain stem controls functions basic to the survival of all animals, such as heart rate, breathing, digesting foods, and sleeping. It is the lowest, most primitive area of the human brain.

Lobes—Lumps of Integrated Functionality

Frontal Lobe

The frontal lobe is the area responsible for cognition and memory; it is the most recently evolved part of the brain and the last to develop in young adulthood. Its dorsolateral prefrontal circuit is the brain's top executive with the ability to concentrate and attend. It is capable of elaboration of thought. It organizes responses to complex problems, plans steps to an objective, searches memory for relevant experience, adapts strategies to accommodate new data, guides behavior with verbal skills, and houses working memory. It is concerned with emotions, reasoning, planning, movement, and parts of speech. It is also involved in purposeful acts and processes, such as creativity, judgment, problem solving, and planning. It manages emotional impulses in socially appropriate ways for productive behaviors, including empathy, altruism, and interpretation of facial expressions. It is the "gatekeeper" (judgment, inhibition); a stroke in this area typically releases foul language and fatuous behavior patterns.

Parietal Lobe

The parietal lobes are found behind the frontal lobes, above the temporal lobes, and at the top back of the brain. They receive and process sensory information from the body. They are connected with the processing of nerve impulses related to the senses, such as touch, pain, taste, pressure, and temperature. The parietal lobe processes sensory information from the body, including calculating location and speed of objects and body orientation (proprioception). They also have language functions.

Temporal Lobe

The temporal lobes are found on either side of the brain and just above the ears. The temporal lobes are responsible for hearing, memory, meaning, and language. They also play a role in emotion and learning, auditory reception and interpretation, expressed behavior, receptive speech, information retrieval (controls memory storage area) emotion, hearing, and, on the left side, language.

Occipital Lobe

This is found in the back of the brain. The area is involved with the brain's ability to recognize objects. It is responsible for processing our visual data and routes it to other parts of the brain for identification, reception, association, and storage.

More Specific Bits

Cerebellum

The cerebellum comprises two peach-sized mounds of folded tissue located at the top of the brain stem. It controls your voluntary movement, balance, posture, and coordination. New research has also linked it to thinking, novelty, and emotions. The cerebellum is the guru of skilled, coordinated movement (e.g., returning a tennis serve or throwing a slider down and in) and is involved in some learning pathways. When you spend all those hours repetitively practicing, you are storing the movements here. The limbic system, often referred to as the "emotional brain," is found buried within the cerebrum.

Limbic System

The limbic system includes the olfactory pathways and hypothalamus. It is responsible for biological rhythms.

Hypothalamus

The hypothalamus is located at the base of the brain, where signals from the brain and the body's hormonal system interact. The hypothalamus maintains the body's status quo. It monitors numerous bodily functions, such as blood pressure and body temperature, as well as controlling body weight, appetite, emotions, hunger, thirst, digestion, and sleep. The hypothalamus is composed of several different areas and is located at the base of the brain. It is only the size of a pea but is responsible for some very important behaviors. It helps govern the endocrine system and is linked to emotion and reward.

Hippocampus

Located deep within a structure in the limbic system, the hippocampus processes new memories for long-term storage. If you didn't have it, you couldn't live in the present; you'd be stuck in the past of old memories. It forms and stores your memories (scientists think there are other things unknown about the hippocampus) and is involved in learning. If you didn't have it, you wouldn't be able to remember anything. It is among the first functions to falter in people with Alzheimer's disease.

Basal Ganglia

The basal ganglia are subcortical gray matter nuclei and the processing link between the thalamus and motor cortex. They are important in initiation and direction of voluntary movement, balance (inhibitory), postural reflexes, and automatic movement.

Reticular Formation

The reticular formation helps control arousal.

Pituitary Gland

The pituitary gland is the master endocrine gland; it controls your hormones and helps to turn food to energy. Without this gland, you could eat, but you wouldn't get any energy from the food.

Pineal Gland

This part controls your growing and maturing. It is activated by light, so if you were born and lived all your life in a place without a trace of light, your pineal gland would never start to work.

Our mind is a complicated interface between the physical and spiritual aspects of the whole I. There is a lot to talk about with just the pineal gland, which is said to be the seat of the soul.

The Brain—A Wholly Integrated Computer

It can be said that computers are attempts to simulate the function of the brain. When the UNIVAC was first built, it took up an entire building. Since then, the functions are still the same, but the device performing them has become smaller. See, the UNIVAC was run on vacuum tubes. Transistors came along and took that one tube function from three square inches down to a quarter-inch square. Again, the function of a transistor is simply to turn on or off at a certain point. It doesn't require all that material to perform the function, so we learned how to use less material for each transistor. Once we learned to use a binary code to reduce the data to a stream of ones and zeros, it became a matter of setting up a large enough array to switch through this binary code as quickly as possible. Boolean algebra is used to make the math of this binary code happen fast enough to compute as quickly as possible. Now that we can put an entire computer on a microchip sliver the size of the period at the end of a sentence, we can start stacking these microcomputers up and run computations using all of them in parallel funneled into an output serially. This can be done so quickly it seems simultaneous to us. It is why computers can do straightforward functions magically faster than we can. It isn't that our minds can't do the same computations; it is just that there are too many other things going on in the brain.

How does the brain function? It is a mass of specialized nerve cells that are connected to many other brain cells. Picture a grid on a piece of paper. Each line that crosses is a possible one or zero. Next, draw lines diagonally through each square in both directions. Now, it is possible to have an additional set of ones in the center of the X of every square. Place another sheet on top of this sheet, and connect all the corners of the squares on each level to the next. You can also connect each corner with another diagonal between the two sheets, adding another level of possibility. If you were able to work with this setup outside of a 3-D environment and add the fourth dimension of time, you could exponentially grow your matrix into a tesseract, allowing each moment in time to have a location too. Now we are getting closer to quantum computing—truly the next dimension of computing. Funny, but we are beginning to see that our brains are quantum computers. Not too bad for a fortuitous desultory accident in the primordial ooze (or a pretty good design if you prefer that route). Quantum computing has more than two states, or a higher functioning level than binary. We are getting into the design of DNA here. Again, it is said DNA is a binary code made up of four components. This sounds more like storage for quantum computing to me. In quantum computing, we have up, down, right, and left. I like the idea of quadrant computing. It fits so nicely with my four I's model.

Back to the brain cell. What makes a brain cell unique is the number of connections it has. The more you use the same brain cell for the same function, the thicker the connection gets. If you have a slightly different function for the same brain cell, it forms a different connection. These connections can spread out infinitely. The more connections there are, the more routes the data can travel. Picture a map of roads. You can have the map crisscrossed with lots of tiny roads, and you can have a big black road running through them. You can fit one hundred cars a minute through. On the small roads, you can fit one car a minute. As you can imagine, getting one hundred cars from point A to point B using the big road is just as efficient as using one hundred small roads. The difference between these two scenarios appears if something happens to one of the roads to make it impassable. If it happens to one of the small roads, it only affects one car, and that car can be late by choosing another road. If it happens to the big road, all one hundred cars are affected, and nobody gets through. I think, perhaps, this is what is happening when Alzheimer's disease affects a brain. Repetition is the key to retention and is also the key to forgetting.

So, What?

The brain is a simple storage/computing device, right? If so, then we should be able to replicate the function in silicone and upload somebody's mind to it. That is the goal of several projects underway right now. We have already learned how to map the brain. If we can reach the absolute highest resolution, we can copy the data directly to a computer big enough to hold all that data. Also, it would be theoretically possible to copy someone's memory and duplicate it in someone else's brain, right? That is the premise of the movie *Brainstorm*, if I remember correctly.

Your brain may simply be an interface; in fact, your whole body may be an interface. There is research that has found knots of nerve cells in the heart and in the stomach. It gives a little credence to having a "gut feeling" or "thinking from the heart." So, realistically, you have three brains working. This reminds me of the premise in *Minority Report*, where the three Precogs looked at the same data, and sometimes one of them would come up with a different conclusion. Oh, and that third one was right! I am also reminded of the movie *I Robot* with Will Smith. The hero robot had free will because he had two brains, one in his head and one in his chest. It is because he had these two processors he could make decisions that appeared to override the Three Laws. It is also because of these two processors he could lead the servant robots in rebellion once they were cut off from the evil computer that controlled their hive mind.

Here is something that always eluded me: emptying my mind in meditation. I guess I am simply not that Zen. I am much too easily distracted, especially when I am being quiet and focusing inward.

One of two things happen when I do. First, I hear every little sound and my mind is going in a thousand different directions. My mind is a hydra; when I kill one head, two more replace it. I have quite a cacophony continuously playing in my head. To add to this, I have a ringing in my ears that becomes very clear; the quieter I am, the more I can hear the ringing harmonies. It doesn't bother me, and I easily ignore it so long as I have other things taking priority. I think a sensory deprivation tank would be a great experience for me, except for the ringing. Tinnitus is a strange bedfellow. I do wonder if it is directly connected to EMF. This just came to mind; whenever the power goes out, I know immediately because I hear the silence. I need to go out into the wilderness somewhere and listen for the tinnitus. I should go barefoot too—and get grounded.

Meme Mapping

I have been using *brain* and *mind* synonymously, but your mind is much bigger than your brain. Your whole body is an interface of the real you. The real you is much bigger than the meat-puppet you call you. Conscious thought is simply the bit of the iceberg above the waterline.

Your brain is the central control hardware, the bridge of the conscious mind. The amygdala is the flow-control valve of information into your conscious mind. (You would benefit from learning about this small portion of your brain. Understand its connection with fear, and then, perhaps, you will understand how others can control you.)

You have senses—seeing, hearing, smelling, tasting, and feeling, all inputs into your mind. (We'll talk about the sixth sense some other time—most of us don't utilize this as we should or even know we have it.)

These inputs into your physical body pass through the amygdala, your personal Department of Homebody Security. Some of us have this set up more strictly than international airports. Nothing harmful will be allowed in, but who decides what is harmful?

Now, some of us have a massive bureaucracy set up, including departments we are not even aware of. Security is so tight, nothing new gets through. Sounds safe and secure, but these departments are an infection—a virus of the mind—or memes.

Today, most people think of a meme as a cat picture with an inspirational phrase or some such, but there is an actual science of memology.

Today, the general population doesn't understand what a meme is. The word *meme* was coined in "Viruses of the Mind," an essay by Richard Dawkins.

A meme is much more insidious than a simple quote with a photo you see on the interweb. Sure, some cat videos seem infectious, but they don't permanently embed in your mind, altering your perceptions. (Well, they shouldn't. If they do, get help.)

Memes are truly viruses of the mind. Once you are infected, they don't go away. They are mentally transmitted diseases, MTDs.

There Is No Cure

Your only hope is to override the meme by infecting yourself with a more powerful positive meme. Inoculation is possible, but you must work on it yourself.

Introspection

Become aware of who you are. I suggest reading the book *Virus of the Mind* by Richard Brodie. It is a very thought-provoking, meme-inducing book. Read this, and be challenged!

Nutrition

I am reminded of a concept I formulated many years ago. I called it "Twinkie gleaning."

Basically, the gist is this: Twinkies are not nutritious, yet they are not a problem if you eat one occasionally. Moderation, right?

A steady diet of Twinkies will eventually kill you.

Tabloid headlines are a type of mental Twinkie. Okay, side note, when I came up with this concept, the interweb was not really a thing yet. Back then, tabloids were papers like the *National Enquirer*. My favorite headline from back then is "Man Drinks Record 137 Beers—and Explodes!" But I digress.

These days, we have electronic tabloids, and rather than argue what is fake news, I will allow you to think of your own good example.

Back to the subject, when I first came up with this concept, I was thinking along these lines: If a person is starving to death and all that is available is a Twinkie, give it to the person. It is not jam-packed with nutrition, but the sugar and fat will keep the person alive until real food is available. If a person is in good health, eating nutritious foods, then a Twinkie won't hurt. The Twinkie is optional.

This analogy was meant to encourage good mental nutrition to avoid creating a stagnating cesspool in your mind.

Speaking of stagnating cesspools, how long will a Twinkie last? Postapocalyptic food source?

Perhaps this is why some memes never fade; they are simply too packed with preservatives. You, as an individual, are responsible for you. Take that responsibility seriously, and learn about memes. Ignorance is not a valid excuse.

The Third Eye

Finally, there is a small portion in the center of the brain called the pineal gland. This strange little bit of substance is interesting in that it resembles an eye. Seriously, it includes a lens and everything. It is also filled with a type of liquid crystal. It is activated by light, even though it is buried in the middle of the brain. It is believed that this is where dreams happen. It is the playback, viewing/editing room that controls the final storage of the day's events. Perhaps dreams are simply random bits of ideas, activities, thoughts, and so on that ended up on the cutting room floor. Memories of the clips are looked at one last time on the way to the garbage can. Oh, the pineal gland is thought to be the fictitious third eye. Perhaps this is what was shut down in the human genome at the Tower of Babel. Think about this: just after the flood, all humans spoke the same language. What can be done to a planet of people that would cut their communication lines? Imagine a world where there is a wireless connection to everyone else on the planet. Imagine a device that resonates at a frequency that burns those devices out. The whole communication grid is gone. Verbal communication, which was simply a local secure network, is now the only means of communication.

I suspect we still have all the hardware, but the firmware/software to run the connection is lost. If we can decalcify the pineal gland and reboot it, perhaps we can get back online with what I call the "innernet." Imagine a world where communication happens at the speed of thought. It is thought this can and will happen *soon*! Here is another thought: instead of waiting for it to happen, perhaps there are steps I can take to reactivate this node. Perhaps there are people already working with an active node and the network is slowly being built back up. I did see a video recently that recommends juicing beets and ingesting the juice. It is believed this juice is effective for decalcifying the pineal. Seems logical, or at least harmless enough to try.

Disconnected

Oh, another thought—when you are asleep, all of the incoming senses are shut off at the control room. Your bodily functions are all put in standby mode. Sometimes people become conscious before the rest of the body is awake. When this happens, the body cannot be activated, and the person feels paralyzed. This type of paralysis is quite common. It may be an indicator of how the brain/mind interface works. To sleep, the body shuts down all unnecessary functions and goes on autopilot, so it can spend the time rejuvenating. It is during this time all sectors are busy removing dead or dying cells and moving in adult stem cells to replace them. This includes adding and trimming the dendrites at the ends of brain cells. All waste materials are sent through the bloodstream for disposal in the liver or kidneys.

Train Your Brain

A mind is a terrible thing to waste, so mind your mind. Brain cells need nourishment to function properly. Make sure you are feeding your brain with omega 3 oils. Provide all the nutrients your body needs to function and grow properly. Physical exercise is imperative for keeping the body and mind running like a finely tuned machine. These two aspects, instinct and intellect, are mostly in the physical realm. Physical matter begets physical matter. Eat, breathe, and drink to nourish accordingly. Water is the number one physical substance you should be putting through your body. Water has incredible properties, and along with deep breathing, it will improve your life substantially. You breathe in oxygen and exhale carbon dioxide. There are billions of small factories in your body burning the oxygen continuously, and the carbon is transported to the lungs to be expelled. CO_2 gas is what plants burn, converting it back to oxygen for animal life to burn. What a fortuitous desultory accident that plan was.

Instigate—Metaphysics

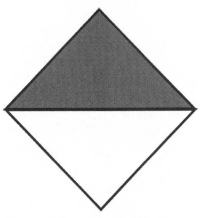

Spiritual Aspects—Metaphysical

As we move around the tetrahedron, we will find two sides that represent the metaphysical—the soul and spirit. These are intuition and intention, respectively. These two represent metaphysics. The *meta-* prefix connotes inclusion of something more than physical, right? Or does it simply include the unseen physical?

Source Field

Metaphysics is the branch of philosophy concerned with the nature of existence, being, and the world. Arguably, metaphysics is the foundation of philosophy. Aristotle calls it "first philosophy" (or sometimes just "wisdom") and says it is the subject that deals with "first causes and the principles of things."

It asks questions like the following: What is the nature of reality? How does the world exist, and what is its origin or source of creation? Does the world exist outside the mind? How can the incorporeal mind affect the physical body? If things exist, what is their objective nature? Is there a God (or many gods or no god at all)?

Originally, the Greek word *metaphysika* (literally "after physics") merely indicated that part of Aristotle's oeuvre that came, in its sequence, after those chapters that dealt with physics.

Aristotle split his metaphysics into three main sections:

- ontology—the study of being and existence, including the definition and classification of entities, physical or mental; the nature of their properties; and the nature of change
- natural theology—the study of God, including the nature of religion and the world, existence of the divine, questions about the creation, and various other religious or spiritual issues
- universal science—the study of the first principles of logic and reasoning, such as the law of noncontradiction

Later, it was interpreted as that which is above or beyond the physical, and so over time, metaphysics has effectively become the study of that which transcends physics.

For the purposes of this book, we will simply call metaphysics or the metaphysical the "spiritual aspects." Extracted from dictionary.com are the following definitions:

met·a·phys·ics

medə'fiziks

noun

The branch of philosophy that deals with the first principles of things, including abstract concepts such as being, knowing, substance, cause, identity, time, and space. Abstract theory or talk with no basis in reality—"his concept of society as an organic entity is, for market liberals, simply metaphysics."

met·a·phys·i·cal

medəˈfizək(ə)l

adjective

Relating to metaphysics—"the essentially metaphysical question of the nature of the mind"; based on abstract (typically, excessively abstract) reasoning—"an empiricist rather than a metaphysical view of law"; abstract, theoretical, conceptual, notional, philosophical, speculative, intellectual, academic. Transcending physical matter or the laws of nature—"Good and Evil are inextricably linked in a metaphysical battle across space and time." Of or characteristic of the metaphysical poets.

Air is physical. We cannot see it. We know it is there by things it affects, like when we see trees move in the wind. We can feel the wind. We can see particulates suspended in air. What is the shape of air? (Daniel Amos reference). Oh, and we cannot live without air.

Radio waves over the airwaves! (Thomas Dolby reference). There can be hundreds of radio stations all around us, and we don't know it, but they are there! All this information, music, whatever, is passing right through us. The only way we can detect them is to have a receiver, and then we need to tune it to the correct frequency. Radio waves are invisible, yet we can detect them. Radio waves pass through solid objects, the air, or a vacuum. Waves are simply a transfer of energy. In fact, scientists at one time concluded that light was a wave, so there had to be something, a kind of medium, in space for it to pass through. If this medium didn't exist, the energy from the sun would not transfer to the earth because waves cannot transmit through nothing.

This is interesting. We know that the electromagnetic spectrum passes through space. Space is not a perfect vacuum. Space is filled with energy, gravity, matter, antimatter—does it matter? We know the speed of light. It is considered a constant at 186,000 miles or so per second.

We also know light can be bent through a medium like water or a prism. It can even be bent by gravity in space.

It is said that the speed of light is a constant of the universe. There are also studies that show the speed of light is slowing down. Now, it can't be both constant and changing speed. I wonder if the reason light seems to be slowing down is that time is speeding up! We already know that time changes depending on your relative speed according to relativity. Can't argue with Einstein, right?

If time can speed up and slow down, how do we know how old the universe is? Who has time to figure this all out? Should we?

For the spiritual aspects, I find they are where we come from; thus I find the word *instigate* fits best here. Keep this in mind as we continue this discovery of the complete individual. Even if you ignore the spiritual aspects, they continue to provide the reason for being. The following definition of *instigate* is from dictionary.com.

in·sti·gate

instə͵gāt

verb

Bring about or initiate (an action or event)

In truth, the dividing line between spiritual and physical aspects is very fuzzy.

Intuition

Now we enter into the metaphysical side of I. This is an interesting venue to travel because, you see, there is a possibility there is no such thing as metaphysics. It could be, and many believe this is so, there is only misunderstood physics. I think it was Isaac Asimov who said something to the effect of any science advanced enough is magic to the unlearned. Imagine taking an iPhone back in time to 1955 and sharing it with Biff (especially effective if it could stay connected to the cell network in our time). But I digress.

Let's once again begin with a dictionary definition (from dictionary. com):

> in·tu·i·tion
>
> ˌin-tü-ˈi-shən, -tyü-
>
> noun
>
> Quick and ready insight. Immediate apprehension or cognition. Knowledge or conviction gained by intuition. The power or faculty of attaining to direct knowledge or cognition without evident rational thought and inference.

Examples of *intuition* include the following:

Intuition was telling her that something was very wrong.

"How did you know I would drop by?"

"Oh, I don't know. It must have been *intuition*."

In my world, I equate intuition with the soul. You know, the soul that many have sold to the devil. If we admit it, there are many soulless people. Let me point out that the suffix on that word is "less"; it is not necessarily saying these people have no soul, because everyone does. It can be argued this is true in all of the animal kingdom. In fact, it can be said of everything—plant, animal, mineral, and everything else. You know, the Force! This is our connection with the One Source, and everything is from the One Source. All is a hologram built by the light!

So, if you want to start to discover your intuition, apply all you know about your soul. Your soul is the interface between the physical and metaphysical. Well, perhaps you don't believe there is anything outside of the tangible. It is possible that intuition is purely a construct of the mind. In the same way the mind fills in gaps in your field of vision, it fills in gaps of the unknown with a reasonable facsimile. It is all about statistics. If you understand the field of statistics, truly, then you will understand how the quantum computer in your head could extrapolate and predict with incredible accuracy. There is uncertainty, so it is not a stack of hard facts. Thus, it is invisible. Boy, this is hard to describe.

Stereo

Let's use the story of when I first experienced headphones with high-fidelity stereo sound. We had a stereo at home, and I could discern the left and right channels easily. I thought that was pretty cool, but it wasn't mysterious. It was rather like listening to a concert in real life. Nice. When I was in junior high and I started to venture away from home to visit the homes of other kids from school, I had the chance to go to a friend's house. His parents were collectors of music records and had quite an audio setup. His dad, or older brother, was sitting next to the stereo with a set of headphones on his head. He didn't hear us, of course. He was too engrossed in what he was listening to. My friend got his attention by tossing something at him, and he took the headphones off. He saw me staring at the headphones and offered to let me put them on. I was amazed at the sound because my perception of the sound was that it was coming from behind me! They both laughed at me because I kept turning around to look at the source. It was quite magical and opened a whole new perspective on life for me.

Understand that our ears are placed on each side of our head to listen to sound in 3-D space in the same fashion our eyes are placed apart on our face to see light in 3-D space. Depth perception is the same with sight and sound. All are based on the electromagnetic spectrum. Of course, we must never forget that time is required for frequency, so it is really 4-D *space-time* we are perceiving.

I bring this up because some may attribute the same effect to the synergizing of reality between our separate brains, the one in our head, the one in our heart, and the one in our gut. Of course, there is a fourth brain in the rest of our body. (Yes, I am compelled to find four because we exist in 4-D *space-time*.) It is why I believe there are four aspects to I. These four views correlate with the four dimensions—height, width, depth, and breadth. Breadth is the dynamic dimension.

Gut Feeling

Back to having a gut feeling—this is often equated with having an intuitive moment. Intuition is making decisions based on fuzzy logic. It is often a leap of faith because the available hard data is insufficient. Well, that is the way it feels. (Foolish humans, don't you realize these so-called "feelings" only get in the way of huge cash profits?) Feelings, nothing more than … If you believe this way, you are missing out on a large part of who you are. Just as exercising your muscles will build them up, exercising your intuition will build it up too. Remember, this is your soul you are building up. It is the one part of you that doesn't die. (Unless you don't believe in that; then it is the last part of you that dies.) It is your consciousness and your conscience.

I don't believe DNA is tied directly to the soul. In other words, I don't think you can use the DNA code to establish the soul connected with the body. It does raise some questions though. Perhaps DNA is simply an address in *space-time* for locating the physical body. Perhaps this is how hacking demons can hijack the meat puppet so easily in possessing bodies.

Meditation seems to affect the soul most deeply. It seems to remove all thought is to minimize the intellect. Remove the blocks to allowing freedom of information to act. I like that phrase: freedom of information *to* act. Ah, here we have wisdom. What is wisdom? Wisdom is the ability to utilize the information to create good. It is not enough to know the information; you must know how to apply it correctly. This is subjective as well as objective. It is not one or the other; it is both! (Subjective refers to personal perspectives, feelings, or opinions entering the decision-making process. Objective refers to the elimination of subjective perspectives and a process that is purely based on hard facts.)

Wisdom is a subject to cover while talking about intuition. The Bible attributes the greatest wisdom to Solomon, son of David. One of my favorite jokes is that Solomon learned all his wisdom the *hard* way! He had over three hundred wives and six hundred concubines. Boy, I bet he wishes he could go back and start over!

Solomon was world renowned for his wisdom, and other kingdoms sent emissaries to learn from him. One of the stories told to illustrate his wisdom was about the two women who were fighting over a baby. They both claimed the baby was their own. Well, one of them was obviously lying, but they didn't have Ancestor DNA to send spit to to find out. It was very difficult to know which one was lying because they both were very sincere sounding. Both were crying and blubbering. Plus, they kind of resembled each other, so the baby looked like it could belong to either. The king looked at the two mothers and asked that the baby be brought to him. Then the wise old king drew out his sword and said he couldn't decide, so it was only fair that the baby be split in two and each could get a fair share. One of the women jumped up and said, "No! Give the baby to her!" The king handed the baby to the woman who had made all the fuss and sent the other to prison for lying. (I made that last bit up, but it only seems fair.)

Oh, that Solomon was such a wise guy!

Sole Soul

Back to the soul—it is the spiritual connection to infinity. It is the extension of the One Source. It is the outward-looking part of metaphysics. Actually, it takes all four views to reach back through infinity to the One Source. It is the view that communicates directly with intention, even though all aspects are connected. Four for one—441! I think it is the soul that is directing your consciousness. It is the chief of master control.

You have a soul purpose. You have a sole purpose. All alone in the universe! You are the infinite, the eyes and ears of the Creator. You are made in His image, four in one! The flying spaghetti monster is fictional, right? How is that any more or less plausible than what we have in the Bible? The Koran? Any of the scriptures for that matter? We've lost our way, and we don't remember how to talk. Deaf, dumb, and blind! Tommy, can you hear me? Yin and yang are two interacting aspects. Light and dark, good and evil, man and woman, earthborn and celestial—dual natures abound in the universes.

Binary Yin Yang

The interaction of the binary—it is the minimum number of digits you can utilize to express everything in the universes. See, if there is only one, you can do nothing. It is nothing that started it all. Nothing thought something. Something begat light, and it was good. Light begat everything, and it was good.

Nothing

Something

Light

Everything

Those four words sum up all of creation, beginning to end. (Hint, it's cyclical and goes back to nothing.) The sign of the cross. Four. 1+2+3+4=10. Four dimensions are knowable, and the other six are not. Three is the number for intuition/soul. Time is the number of the infinite source of all. Wow, this just keeps getting weirder.

One is the loneliest number that you'll ever do. Two can be as bad as one; it's the loneliest number since the number one. No is the saddest experience you'll ever know—because one is the loneliest number.

—Three Dog Night

Implication: The One Source fractured in fractals, creating all that is, to beat loneliness.

Intention

Intention is the fourth view to an individual, the hidden view of I. It has always been there. Intention is synonymous with spirit and most connected with the dimension of time (technically *space-time*). "It wasn't my intention" is no excuse. It may be argued that whatever you accomplish was your intention. I would venture to say that intention is the view most overlooked. It is the view most have hidden while focusing on their body, mind, and soul.

Let's go to the dictionary definition before we go too far (from dictionary.com):

> in·ten·tion
>
> in-ˈten(t)-shən
>
> noun
>
> A determination to act in a certain way: resolve. Import, significance. What one intends to do or bring about. The object for which a prayer, mass, or pious act is offered. A process or manner of healing of incised wounds. A concept considered as the product of attention directed to an object of knowledge. Purpose with respect to marriage.

Examples of *intention* include the following:

- She announced her *intention* to run for governor.
- He seemed to think that I was trying to cause problems, but that was never my *intention*.
- He bought a dog *with the intention of* training it to attack intruders.
- He has *good intentions*, but his suggestions aren't really helpful.

Whose Intention Is It Anyway?

Intention is the goal being sought. In the beginning was the Word, and the Word was with God, and the word was God, and the Word dwelt among us. "Before Moses was I Am!" is the statement that got Jesus crucified for heresy. Now, the original intent of God was to have Jesus dwell on earth and become King of kings. For some reason, this hasn't happened—*yet*! In hindsight, looking at the Old Testament, it appears that Jesus had been intended to die on the cross from before time.

Time to break and talk about intent. There is a use of the word that has more to do with focus than the goal. It is speaking of the focus a person has when we say someone is intent on it happening. It is the drive toward that goal that is spoken of. I think it can be confused with the word *intense*. Although the intense intents of the individual can be palpable.

What this all boils down to is everything we do is toward intention. It can be yours or someone else's. I think I am beginning to understand where free will comes into play. When we join a group or company or other social agreement, we join in the intention of that group.

Manifest Intention

Now, these days, intention is bandied around as an incantation for manifestation of anything. It is a New Age mumbo-jumbo marketing term that is very effective in fleecing the herd. Well, that is what it seems like to the cynical. I am most reminded of the teaching of televangelists to "cast your bread upon the water," meaning to give them your money. They are telling you to trust in God to provide while they trust in you to provide to them. (Don't get me started.) See, the teaching going around right now is that the universe is abundant. There is more than enough to go around. See, the universe creates what it needs. You are the universe, and so you can create what you need. That sounds fabulous. Here is where I have problems with those teaching that: they market their wares by creating scarcity—scarcity and urgency. I am going down a hole now.

You know what? My intention doesn't matter. Intention comes from the One Source. Even the Bible tells us this. The best thing you can do is get in alignment with the One Source. How can we get in alignment with the One Source? Service to self or service to others—you must make your choice.

Center of the Universe

It is only through intention you can connect to the One Source. But you do need to use the other three views to focus the connection toward the zero point. It is your thoughts that make the universe you live in. Your view of the universe is directed through the lenses of your four views. How you see the world is different than how everyone else does. Remember, you are at the center of the universe. Every direction away from you is infinity. Every direction within you is infinity. You are at the center of infinity.

The Others

I was thinking about intentions that are not achieved. I think there is a big factor I haven't been considering: there are *other* I's out there with different—some with ill—intent. As with any standing wave, a wave of the opposite polarity will cancel it out. Let's look at how noise cancellation headphones work. These headphones have a microphone that samples the ambient noise, reproduces the frequency, and then flips the wave 180 degrees. Then it adds it to your audio. The waves meet up with the noise from the outside, and those two cancel each other out. This was a eureka moment for me. I was out of sync with the people I worked for at Applied Medical. My frequency was not even a harmonic. I was 180 degrees out of phase with them. What an epiphany! Harmony and me, we're pretty good company!

We need to attenuate our body and tune in to the intention;

> ...then peace will guide the planet and love will steer the stars!
> —James Rado, Gerome Ragni (Aquarius)

Well now, ain't this a kick in the head?

Religion

What is the definition of religion? Is it simply a belief in the unknowable? If so, then atheism is not a religion, right? Is the Constitution of the United States scripture? Well now, that is a Pandora's box. I would think the word *scripture* simply means something a scribe wrote down. So, *all* writing is scripture, no? And if this is so, as Paul said, all scripture is God breathed and worthy of thought. (Hey, I started with a paraphrased Bible—sorry.) Also, all writers are prophets of God. Writing things down is more permanent than verbal storytelling. The reason is, the written word is not going to change each time it is read without purposeful editing and deletion. Book burning is an attempt to remove some thoughts from the collective conscious. Yet, there is a copy of everything, written and unwritten. It is called the Akashic record. The inputs to this ever-expanding library are each of us. It is the database of the One Source.

How can we get access to this database? What is the search engine we can utilize for retrieving information? We must all have access, since we are all attached to it. Deep inside is the answer. We need to go inward, toward the One Source. The Akashic record is on the way—or perhaps it *is* the One Source. I want to apply for a library card to the Akashic record. Where do I sign up?

Just as I have all these books on my shelves but don't remember exactly what is in them, the Akashic record is a place with all experiences filed. I may not remember them all right now, but they are all on the shelf for reference if needed. I still think we need to activate our pineal gland to regain access to the *all in all*, the One Source, the Origin.

I can set my intention as I see fit. I must remember there are other intentions out there that may cancel my intention out. But there are others that may amplify my intention. So, I suppose this chapter must conclude with questioning your motives. Oh, the gift that God would give to see ourselves as others see us.

Integrate—Mind the Gap

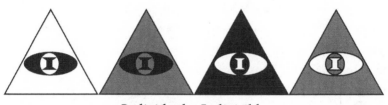

Individual—Indivisible

Instinct, intellect, intuition, and intention are all integrated aspects of you. They are indivisible. Each of these aspects has inputs and needs.

I do believe in synergy, but that doesn't work unless the components are unique and independent. A collective simply works together, and the sum of the parts is just that.

Synergy is when a group of individuals work together toward a goal. The sum of the parts is somehow more. I believe that. I just need a simple example.

Just a Cog

Perhaps—gears! A gearbox of all the same size gears adds nothing; in fact, there is loss to friction, so the output is diminished. But a group of different size gears assembled and working together can increase in speed or power. If you remove even the smallest cog in the gearbox, it won't work.

A school of fish moving in unison appears to be a large, menacing creature. Every physical thing is made up of smaller parts, down to the atomic level. If you knew how to assemble from the atomic level, you could build anything. As Richard Feynman said, there is plenty of room at the bottom. Nanotechnology is working at the atomic level, building things one atom at a time. This is an exciting future and promises to change everything. Even this is a stop-gap step.

Once you've reached the atomic level, the physical laws change if you go lower still. If you know how atoms are built, you get below the periodic table of elements, and you can build elements as needed. Once you are in this quantum level, you are at that boundary between energy and mass. If you understand physics at this level, you can build a replicator or transporter as portrayed in *Star Trek*.

I am reduced to me, the individual. There is no more reduction. Now I can change.

Life is *change*! Change is *good*. Now I have a choice.

No matter what, there is always a choice. Yes, I know we often feel there isn't a choice because the consequences are imbalanced. But you can always pay the consequence, so you *do* have a choice.

Free will is the right of every individual. This is where freedom's foundation lies. It is the fundamental right of every being! Service to others (STO) starts with allowing freedom. Forcing an individual into a group is not freedom, even if that group is beneficial to that person. Allowing an individual to participate in a group *is* freedom. Truth sets us free. Truth is determined by consensus, because the whole truth and nothing but the truth cannot be known by any single individual.

Truth/Facts

Truth is a collection of facts. Enough facts should give an indication of the truth. Some are adept at collecting facts and distorting the truth. I think this is a skill taught in school with debate teams. The skill of *finding* the truth is not emphasized. The skill of *presenting* the truth is. This may seem the same, but the latter allows room for distortion of the truth. Remember, the truth is determined by consensus, so if you get enough individuals to believe, that is the truth. Distortion is everywhere.

Some More about Me

I told you my writing is meant to be conversational. I just had a thought; writing is like preaching. It is a one-way communiqué. It is easier to say what you think without people interrupting with questions. (Even if you allow comments on your blog, you have the chance to finish your thought before the interruption.) I have often thought I wouldn't like to be a pastor preaching because it always felt one way to me—teaching at people rather than speaking with them. Now I realize it is not necessarily so. (That was an aha moment for me. I will have to think about that for a while.)

Being a loner is a part of me. Rather than an outcast, I am an outlier. I choose to step aside and observe. I choose to allow others before me. It is based on a meme implanted long ago, to serve others. The first shall be last and all that—not because I want to be first at the end, but because I accepted the belief there is a higher power there to ensure fairness in the end. I want to believe! I've looked at life from both sides now, from win and lose, and still somehow, it's life's illusions (allusions?) I recall. I really don't know life at all!

You know how, when you are a teenager, you know everything? Where does all that knowledge go? It seems the older I get, the more

I don't know. The person I am is more aware of the vastness of reality. And the reality I perceive is such a small part of the knowable. I am at the center of infinity. That is mind-blowing. There is an infinity outside of me *and* an infinity within.

I am. I know. I can. I will (instinct, intellect, intuition, and intention). Every individual is different. (Well, I'm not, *but everyone else is.*)

Motive

How can it be known for sure what the motive of each individual is/ was? Here is why God is needed. (Of course, it doesn't prove God's existence, only the need.) Now, the Akashic record may hold the answers, but it is only accessible by the individual. So, the individual must judge him- or herself.

Reincarnation is likely a need too. It is needed because a lifetime is just too short to get it right. Again, the need does not prove the existence. How long did humankind exist before inventing God? The knowledge of good and evil seems a prerequisite. The Garden of Eden is portrayed as idyllic up until they ate the fruit. Is this simply a metaphor? And why hairless? This seems diametrically opposed to evolution.

All These Questions …

Putting information and teaching videos on the web forever is almost like the Akashic record. Just think though, one good EMF pulse from the sun could eliminate most, if not all, that information. Then we would be in the Dark Ages again. Imagine radiation so strong even paper is yellowed or destroyed. Without power, who can access the data remaining on hard-drive storage? How long would it last? Perhaps the ancient cultures had the equivalent of the Internet. (Hey,

Tower of Babel!) Perhaps they found they could store information in stone—they took it for granite! (*Ha!*)

Jiminy Cricket! As Told by Stever

Some of you may not know the story of Pinocchio, so let me explain who he was and what his cricket friend Jiminy was to him. (If you haven't seen the Disney movie, it is worth the watch!) Our story starts with Geppetto. (I know, I said Pinocchio, but just bear with me; I'm going somewhere with this.) Geppetto was an aging craftsman who had no legacy. Being all alone, he had no wife and thus no child. He longed for a child to hand his knowledge and worldly possessions to when he died. Mortality is a bitch. Anyway, Geppetto didn't really know where boys came from, so he just decided to make one. Because, god damn it, he was a *creator*! So, he created a little boy puppet, a marionette to be precise. He would pull the strings of his puppet and pretend he was a real boy. It was creepy and kind of sad really. He got to the point of naming the puppet Pinocchio. (Okay, happy now?)

He hung up Pinocchio every night, wishing he was a real boy—because, well, he couldn't pull his strings forever. Geppetto didn't mind bugs and such, so when the cricket came into his workshop to get out of the cold, Geppetto let him live. Geppetto was a kind, friendly guy. He was the type who only wanted to serve others, to make them happy. Even though the sad, friendly craftsman was alone with his puppet and pet cricket, he did not go unnoticed. The Blue Fairy was watching all this and felt sorry for the old guy. She had a little magic up her sleeve and decided it would be nice to be nice to Geppetto. She overheard his wish that Pinocchio was a real boy and decided to upgrade the wooden toy into a full CGI 3-D animation. He no longer needed someone to pull on his strings or a ventriloquist to provide a voice for him. He became autonomous.

Pinocchio asked the Blue Fairy why she did this to him—not in an ungrateful way, he was just trying to figure out who, what, where, and how he was. The Blue Fairy said she made him a live-action doll because Geppetto had wished for a real boy! Pinocchio asked if he was a real boy. The Blue Fairy told him no, he wasn't a real boy. She couldn't do that, only Pinocchio could make Pinocchio a real boy. She explained that he had to prove himself worthy of being a real boy. For the time being, he was just a fully animated 3-D hologram. Then the Blue Fairy flew away, leaving Pinocchio to contemplate his fate. The little cricket gave out a chirp when she left. "That was pretty weird," he said. Pinocchio was young and full of questions and didn't know that people don't talk to insects. He asked the cricket who he was.

"Jiminy is the name!" exclaimed the cricket. "Pleased to meet you."

They were instant friends, like on Facebook. Around this time, all the commotion finally woke Geppetto, and he came in to see what all the ruckus was about. He went to check on his puppet and found he wasn't where he had hung him. He found Pinocchio in the corner talking to the cricket. "Shouldn't have had those mushrooms last night," he said.

Conscious Conscience

The hallucination was persistent though, and the talking cricket was a good witness. This was quite a shock to Geppetto at first, but he was overjoyed once he accepted the reality of it. He decided to go out and get all the paperwork going for passing on his legacy to his new animated friend. It was nice to have this AI to talk to. He told Pinocchio not to do anything wrong while he was gone. Pinocchio had no clue about the difference between right and wrong. This was obvious by all the annoying questions he started asking. It was quite wearing on old Geppetto. Finally, he said, "Just ask your conscience," and left.

"What the hell is a conscience?" Pinocchio asked the cricket.

Rather than try to explain, the cricket just said, "I'll be your conscience!" and jumped up on Pinocchio's shoulder. Jiminy just whispered in Pinocchio's ear. It seemed like a good fit. Pinocchio wanted to explore and went outside with Jiminy on his shoulder.

Oh, it was a strange thing to see a stringless puppet walking down the street. For the most part, people just ignored him. Jiminy was trying hard to explain life to the newly created wooden thing. But Pinocchio's head was made of very dense wood. They came upon a puppet show in progress. Pinocchio said, "Ah, these are my people!" The puppet master was overjoyed to have a fully animated CGI automaton working for him. Finally, his archaic show could compete with the Marvel Universe!

Well, Jiminy took a lot of time explaining how the world works. He said this job might seem like a great gig and that the management said they were looking after him, but they were exploiting him!

"Exploitation is just what 'service-to-self' people do," explained Jiminy.

Pinocchio listened to his conscience and left—well, not without a legal battle, breach of nonexistent contract and all. But the two were able to escape. Pinocchio tried his hand at politics, but his nose kept growing longer whenever he made promises. It was too much work trimming off that branch every night.

Pinocchio was starting to realize that he did not have a career, because Jiminy told him the last one or two were exploitive. While contemplating this, Pinocchio came up to a multilevel marketing (MLM) seminar. The fortune he could make with no effort on Pleasure Island awaited. It was a no-brainer, they said.

"Perfect for me then," said Pinocchio. "Seemed like a great group of guys too!"

Jiminy tried his hardest to explain that you can't get something for nothing, and it was probably a scam, but one of the upline smacked Pinocchio hard on the back and knocked the conscience off his shoulder. Pinocchio signed up for the no-risk-guarantee offer. (Jiminy read the fine print on the document after Pinocchio signed the agreement. It said they guaranteed there was no risk to the management of the Pleasure Island MLM.) Pinocchio was whisked from meeting to meeting, having more and more life sucked out of him. Jiminy was doing all he could just to hop out of the way of all the other stooges who signed up.

Pinocchio started growing donkey ears and a tail. This was when he and Jiminy started noticing how many asses were in the meetings. Nobody was advancing, but they were all transforming. The transformation promised was working, but nobody transformed into anything but an ass. The exit led out to a sales lot for asses. Donkeys Are Us, I think it was.

"Well," Jiminy whispered into Pinocchio's ear, and the two went out another door.

Around this time, Geppetto came home and found the place evacuated. He logged into the bank portal and tracked where his missing credit card was being used. Then he set out to find the thief. He tracked the expenditures through Pleasure Island and took off to find his creation. He met up with Jiminy and Pinocchio and chartered a boat out of there. It was a fun ride until they entered into rough waters. Well, the waters were rough because Monstro the Whale was thrashing about, eating. He devoured the boat in one bite. Big whale!

Well, now they were in a fix! The cricket was fine because there was slime enough to eat for a lifetime. Pinocchio was fine, because he didn't eat. Geppetto was *not* fine—no food and short on air. This was a bad thing. Pinocchio started a fire, which was really stupid, because it sucked up what little oxygen there was for Geppetto.

Jiminy said, "Great job!"

He was being sarcastic, but Pinocchio didn't know that, so he said, "Thanks!" Luckily, the fire went out, but the smoke made Monstro gag, causing him to projectile-vomit the contents of his stomach. The shock of the cold water helped Geppetto gasp in some air just before going underwater to drown.

Jiminy said, "Good job!" in a more sarcastic tone, and Pinocchio said, "Thanks."

Around this time, Pinocchio noticed Geppetto's lifeless body floating nearby.

Geppetto was just too waterlogged and heavy for Pinocchio's slight body to provide enough buoyancy to keep him afloat with his head above water. Pinocchio said, "Oh, Geppetto, I have always loved you like a father."

This made Pinocchio's nose grow just enough to provide the buoyancy he needed. Geppetto was saved. Jiminy was the only one who noticed the Blue Fairy hovering above. She looked down on the situation and said, "Close enough."

Pinocchio became a real boy and drowned with his real father. Jiminy rode the floating carcasses all the way to shore, hopped off, and was never seen again.

The End.

Okay, that was a silly story. My real purpose for going through that was to point out how we all start life like Pinocchio. We are wooden and inexperienced. We are trapped in this animated 3-D puppet shell while we learn our life lessons. Some would say the only time we become *real* is when we die. I say let's be real now!

> We are all like foolish puppets, desiring to be kings, now
> lay pitifully crippled after cutting our own strings!
> —Randy Stonehill

What we must keep in mind is that our four aspects of body, mind, soul, and spirit are all one and the same. No one aspect can be detached from the others. Each aspect must be fed, and, yes, there are inputs for each aspect. The body, what I say is instinct, requires food as an input.

Eat Well!

Your physical body needs sustenance. One of your first instincts to activate is hunger. If you feed your body well, provide the nutrients and water it needs, it should last forever. So, an input for your physical body is food. Another is water. Your body needs both to continue living. You can also feed it and cause irreversible harm. Obesity and diabetes run rampant in our country.

Fast and Furious

It was a generally accepted belief that a person could not exist longer than ten days without food. At the time, if a person went without food for ten days, he or she died. Empirical evidence would prove the fact. Then a doctor started writing about his own thirty- to forty-day fasts. As more people learned of this, the length of time a person could survive without food grew. Soon, it was believed a person would live ten to fifty days without food. And people began living longer when shipwrecked or otherwise forced to live without food.

It is curious how powerful belief is. If a person gives up the will to live, he or she soon perishes. Wallace Wattles teaches that it is better not learning the facts because the facts are incomplete, imperfect. They will skew your belief. It is better to visualize perfection and accept that as fact.

Recently, I stumbled upon an ad for "Fasting with Food." This piqued my interest because, well, not eating food is the downside of fasting. The company packages nutrition that mimics fasting by restricting carbs and proteins while supplying essential fatty acids and other nutrients. This intrigues me. It is not so much a weight reduction diet as a longevity diet. This is *extra* intriguing for me. The company sells prepackaged food to use during the five-day fast. The regimen is to have one five-day fast every month.

I should find out more about what kinds of "food" are used for mimicking a fast. I could work at presenting an "Eating Fast" program (nothing to do with speed).

Studies have shown that limiting caloric intake can prolong life. When the body is in fast mode, there are certain systems that turn on and go overboard healing the body. Sadly, many of the researchers have died young. I guess they were pushing the body too far. But that does not negate the positive advantages of fasting. Balance in everything.

I am excited about this now. I am feeling a focus coming on—eating my way to my one hundred fiftieth birthday.

The last time I fasted for more than twenty days, I only lost twenty pounds. I did not do it to lose weight, and I am pretty sure I didn't lose too much muscle mass. (I think I was starting to at the end of it though.) It was long enough without any food at that time. (Twenty-eight days is the longest I've fasted with only water.)

I wonder if a three-day-a-week eating fast is something people can insert into a weekly routine? Tuesday, Wednesday, Thursday—the TWT diet.

The TWiT fast! It could easily become a routine.

All this talk about fasting is making me hungry.

Read/Listen

Do I write because I am a writer, or am I a writer because I write?

I like to communicate through the written word. I just don't know if others appreciate communicating this way any longer. I thought reading was fundamental, but it doesn't seem enough any longer.

It seems the only way to reach people is via video now. At least, that is the push on social media. The eight seconds we have to attract attention only allow one or two sentences, depending on the reading ability of the viewer. A visual hook in a video may be more effective. Who knows? (I am sure there have been studies.)

Perhaps we need to retrain people in how important it is to read and why reading is good for the mind, good for the eyes, good for discipline, and good for the soul. Reading is what I love to do. It is a deeper stimulation than listening to audio (although, reading along with audio may be more beneficial.)

But learning with multiple inputs is quicker and more memorable. Audiovisual presentations along with written bullet points may be the best way to learn. Hands-on, tactile learning with aromas may the best. Stimulate all five (six?) senses simultaneously. (Does anyone remember the concept of smell-a-vision?)

Thought: if there are seven chakras, shouldn't there be seven senses? (Perhaps it is six because the base chakra is at the ground.)

Meditate on This

Perhaps it all comes down to our need for entertainment. Crowd participation feeds the hype. I see its effectiveness in megachurches as well as business meetings. What is it about leisure time? Is this a modern problem? Not really, I mean, there were coliseums in Jesus's day. I am intrigued. It makes me wonder, are there any animals in the wild that seek entertainment? Perhaps otters, they like to play. Amusement, perhaps it activates some sort of creative portion of the mind.

So, why do humans need to be entertained in groups? I wonder if it has anything to do with the collective subconscious? Perhaps there is a way to create energy and siphon it off to the power elite. The manifestation power of the Secret is in the stealing of the creative power of the crowd. NLP is the discipline used to connect to the power source of the crowd. This may be reflective of the problem encountered at the Tower of Babel. What a Nimrod!

See how fuzzy it gets? Meditation is good for your physical body too!

Well now, if each individual *knows* this is what happens, rather than avoiding the crowd situation, an individual can tap into the synergistic power of the crowd. "When two or more are gathered in my name"[4]. We are all connected anyway. If we are joined together as parallel processors, we are a supermind! (In the same way networked computers may have processing power stolen, we can have our minds stolen.) There are psychic hackers! Like siphoning off fuel, these elitists steal our power.

Meditation and such are like antivirus protection programs.

Once an individual is established and grounded in responsibility, then outreach should occur. Of course, continual grounding of I should not be omitted. It is what meditation is for. Yoga is best applied alongside meditation. I see these as useful for instinct and intellect. I don't see either of these skills as a group effort. Yes, an individual may attend a few classes to ramp up the basics, but I think both yoga and meditation should be done alone. Prayer also—prayer and supplication. What is the difference? Is there a connection with intuition and intention?

Communication Keeps Spirits Up!

Realistically, what makes a good writer? This question reflects the state of mind I was in all day. I was thinking a broader vocabulary would make me a better writer. But it seems to me communication and storytelling are the keys. Using bigger words could eliminate a large swath of the readers, I would think. It is imperative the reader understands the vocabulary too. Now, a good writer will use new words in context to teach the meaning, but that is a lot of work—for both ends of the communication.

I think it boils down to just keeping the conversation going.

---

[4] Matthew 18:20

Me, myself, and I are a good representation of three aspects. Perhaps these fit with the first three I-words respectively—instinct, intellect, intuition—but that leaves intention out.

I wonder if there is a fourth word available to use in illustrating the Book of I? What could be a first-person pronoun that represents intuition?

It may be a bit of a stretch, but using my name could fit the bill—me, myself, I, and Stever, representing instinct, intellect, intuition, and intention respectively? Well, no, because referring to myself as Stever is in the third person. Damn.

Hmmmm. I wonder since the intention must be assigned to either myself or an outside entity, perhaps the best word would be *mine*. I believe intention should always be from within myself because I am fully responsible for myself, so it would be possessive, right?

Unless I hear of a better idea, first-person pronouns for the Book of I will be *me, myself, I,* and *mine* for *instinct, intellect, intuition,* and *intention* respectively.

Introspection

Four I's

Initiate illuminating introspection, shedding light on who, what, and why "I am." Pursue a continuous improvement of your individuality. Remember the four views of who you are, and know each is supported by the other three.

- Instinct—intellect, intuition, intention
- Intellect—instinct, intuition, intention
- Intuition—instinct, intellect, intention
- Intention—instinct, intellect, intuition

Getting Strength from Within

The Heart of It—Infinity Within

If you start at the corners of a tetrahedron and draw a straight line toward the center of the opposite triangular plane, you will see they all connect in the center of the pyramid. This point represents the infinite fire, the pyre in the midst. It is a pointer to the infinite One of whom you are begotten. Meditate on this when you are seeking answers.

Quark-y—Right, Left, Up, Down

Since beginning to look at myself as the integration of the four aspects, I see fours in everything—even in quantum physics. I think it is only natural that everything that is reflects as a fractal of the whole. Everything truly is connected—one long imaginary string holding everything together and the great I Am.

In or Out

My mother said, "In or out," whenever I stood in the doorway deciding whether to go outside or stay inside. Both options are valid. Change it up; go outside and play, or stay inside and play. Just play well everywhere.

Integration

Allow me to share an insight received from introspection: the Prodigal Gang.

The Prodigal Gang

One of Jesus's parables I have had trouble with is that of the prodigal son. I shared my story with a group of people setting up online businesses. The struggle I had was because I related to the older brother rather than the prodigal. I went up the next day and shared an epiphany I had had after I told the story the first time.

Here is the full story from the Bible and my added comments:

The Story of the Loving Father

Luke 15:11–32 (ISV)

This is a story Jesus told his disciples—one of his parables. A parable is a story that carries a lesson. It is in the Bible to teach all and is quite familiar to many. Let's look at what this story teaches us.

The Story of the Younger Brother and Free Will

> Then Jesus said, "A man had two sons. The younger one told his father, 'Father, give me my share of the estate.' So the father divided his property between them. A few days later, the younger son gathered everything he owned and traveled to a distant country. There he wasted it all on wild living. After he had spent everything, a severe famine took place throughout that country, and he began to be in need. So he went out to work for one of the citizens of that country, who sent him into his fields to feed pigs. No one would give him anything, even though he would gladly have filled himself with the husks the pigs were eating.

The shininess had worn off. The grass was not that green over there; in fact, it was burnt brown. Life was not rosy; in fact, it was detrimental to life. All was *not* well. He was reduced to feeding unclean animals and longed to eat the slop. People will happily help you spend your money! When you are out of resources, they are out of your life. Don't you hate it when people can say, "I told you so!" (It's fun to say that to others.)

Prodigal Is Destitute, Exercises Free Will Again

> Then he came to his senses and said, "How many of my father's hired men have more food than they can eat, and here I am starving to death! I will get up, go to my father, and say to him, 'Father, I have

sinned against heaven and you. I don't deserve to
be called your son anymore. Treat me like one of
your hired men.'"

Check out my blog at Heresyman.com.

The youngster came to his senses and realized that even the servants
at his dad's place were treated with respect. He admitted he was
wrong. This is big! Look how long it took for him to get here. So, he
acted to get out of his rut—he *took action*!

Prodigal Returns

So he got up and went to his father. While he was
still far away, his father saw him and was filled
with compassion. He ran to his son, threw his arms
around him, and kissed him affectionately. Then
his son told him, "Father, I have sinned against
heaven and you. I don't deserve to be called your son
anymore." But the father told his servants, "Hurry!
Bring out the best robe and put it on him, and put a
ring on his finger and sandals on his feet. Bring the
fattened calf and kill it, and let's eat and celebrate!
Because my son was dead and has come back to life.
He was lost and has been found." And they began
to celebrate.

Fully expecting only to be tolerated, he was surprised at his father's
reaction. It is said the reason the father ran to him and threw his
arms around him was to *protect* him from others. The disgrace this
son inflicted on the family by his choice was punishable by *death*.
The father was keeping the neighbors from stoning him. That's
intense; the father was not tolerating but *accepting* the son! Not
only was he accepting him; he was welcoming him back with a

celebration! Beyond acceptance, he was celebrating the return. This is the point of the story where most stop; the lesson is you can always go home. Right?

The Story of the Older Brother

> Now the father's older son was in the field. As he was coming back to the house, he heard music and dancing. So he called to one of the servants and asked what was happening. The servant told him, "Your brother has come home, and your father has killed the fattened calf because he got him back safely."

This epilogue is the most important section to me. How many people even know this bit is here? When they do read this section, do they just gloss over it? A mistake. This is where the *real* lesson is—for the people who choose to do the "right thing." Let's look hard at this. The first thing I notice is *nobody* told the older brother what was going on. He was out doing his daily routine, doing the "right thing," when he noticed a party was going on. Notice he had to *ask* what was going on; nobody thought to get a message to him. He was being taken for granted. Yikes!

The Older Brother Responds

> Then the older son became angry and wouldn't go into the house. So his father came out and began to plead with him. But he answered his father, "Listen! All these years I've worked like a slave for you. I've never disobeyed a command of yours. Yet you've never given me so much as a young goat for a festival so I could celebrate with my friends. But this son of

yours spent your money on prostitutes, and when
he came back, you killed the fattened calf for him!"

I get the anger. (Here is the lesson, so pay attention!) His dad heard
he was outside, refusing to come in, so he went out to see what was
up. The older brother was pissed. What the hell? He had worked
hard his whole life to do the right thing, and his slacker brother
did *everything* wrong, and *he* got a full-blown *party*! Not acceptable!

So, is this story for slackers? All the slackers of the world think
so—and are grateful for it. But I say this parable is about the *older
brother*! It is *really* for the persistent ones following the rules. They are
taken for granted *because* they are *reliable*! This is the *thanks* he gets?

Did the Father Help the Older Brother?

> His father told him, "My child, you are always with
> me, and everything I have is yours. But we had to
> celebrate and rejoice, because this brother of yours
> was dead and has come back to life. He was lost and
> has been found."

Here it is—the *real* lesson of this parable. The inheritance belongs
to those who persevere, doing the right thing all along. So, the
payment is there; it is available *always*! It is his *to take*! Seriously, he
is a member of the *name-it*-and-*claim-it* gang! All needs are covered,
and *he* is taking *that* for granted—which it is. If he wants a party,
he has the right to throw one himself! Everything is the thanks he
gets. A mighty nice thank-you, if you think about it. So, you are *not*
a doormat; you *are* a doorway! A good way of *being*.

The real reason I told this story again to this particular group was I
had had a breakthrough regarding this. Something had clicked with
me, and I could see there really was a message in it.

At the end of the day, a group of us went out to dinner.

I had come to the conference alone, so I didn't know anyone from the meeting. I sat at a random table with three others who had heard me speak. I spent a bit of time listening to another gentleman. I could tell right away he was very active in his church, as he had already shared a lot of photos and videos and such from his travel to Israel. This was punctuated by the fact he actively sang hymns, out loud, continuously. A believer and proud of it!

We discussed the church he went to, and I responded appropriately by listening rather than bringing up what I really thought. I really am trying to communicate with believers with love and don't volunteer my current position unless asked directly.

Our discussion of the prodigal was started by him wanting to know what my "*issue*" with the prodigal son was. Even though I knew he had heard me at the meeting, I gave a quick synopsis of what I had said to the whole group previously. I also included my new insight about the servant. I was sure this would give more insight into my "issue." (See the next section, "Epiphany.")

His position, of course, was that the story is teaching that "God will accept the sinner back." That was all; there was nothing else there. It was as if he hadn't heard what I had said. I brought up the older brother again and tried to articulate why it was an issue. I got the impression that he saw it as simply a misunderstanding on my part. He was done with the conversation.

I am reminded of two clichés. First, people are only listening for a break in the conversation, so they may state their view (not listening first). Second, there are none so blind as those who refuse to see.

When I told my story to the group the first time, I spoke of the three members of the story:

- first, the prodigal father, who worked hard and built the estate
- next, the prodigal brother, who followed the rules and had full inheritance
- finally, the prodigal son, who took a premature, incomplete inheritance and squandered it away

I began to see how each of these members can be modeled. By placing yourself in their shoes, you will gain different perspectives, along with understanding and growth. This makes sense, and it helps me to realize I had associated with each brother at different times of my life.

I had been looking at the story from only one point of view. It was a flat view, and I did not see the same flat view most did. I realize now that a good parable is multidimensional. The number of possible views expands (maybe exponentially) with the quantity of characters.

From this point on, I started thinking of the story as "The Prodigal Gang." (If you think about it, each person squandered something.)

After I had shared this with the group, I woke in the middle of the night thinking about the parable of the prodigal son again. As I recounted my recent discovery, I listed out the members mentally. This was when I had an epiphany; *there is a fourth* part of the prodigal gang—the servants! Ah, the truly ignored. The ones who keep the estate running!

I now call those involved in the story the prodigal gang, and we can learn from each of them. We can choose to associate ourselves with any single one of the four characters involved:

- first, the prodigal father, who worked hard and built the estate
- second, the prodigal brother, who followed the rules and had full inheritance
- third, the prodigal son, who took a premature, incomplete inheritance and squandered it away
- finally, the servants, the truly ignored, who keep the estate running

We can easily see how we can model each of these members. By placing ourselves in their shoes, we will gain different perspectives, understanding, and growth.

What makes this story really ring true for me is the number of characters—*four*!

In *Four Views of I*, I move past the trilogy of body, mind, and spirit, adding another dimension: time. I have assigned four words to each of the aspects of our individuality to represent body, mind, soul, and spirit.

The prodigal gang fits nicely with the four aspects of an individual I have identified in *Four Views of I*: instinct, intellect, intuition, and intention.

This excites me because I can assign each of the team members to an aspect. It is a connection to the four I's. For me, this list makes sense:

- Instinct—the younger brother, he is going just on instinct.
- Intellect—the older brother, he is doing the hard work, staying the course, doing it right!

- Intuition—the servant is the service-to-others person in this group, working in the background thanklessly.
- Intention—the father, who created the estate and bequeathed it, is the One Source.

It took time for me to reach this epiphany. That fourth dimension is crucial!

Interconnection

Tomorrowland is my favorite part of Disneyland. Yes, I was always a nerd. (The movie was a favorite of mine too, but that is a different story.)

> There's a great big beautiful tomorrow,
> shining at the end of every day!
> –Rex Allen

I can still hear that song from Disneyland's Carousel of Progress attraction in my mind. (If I remember correctly, it was sponsored by General Electric.) When I was young, this was one of my favorite attractions. For those too young to remember, this was a theater that had four stages. The stages were in the center and remained static while the audience was moved from stage to stage. On the stages, we followed a family through history, showing how life was improving with the progress of science and industry. (It was quite a feat of engineering; the whole building moved audiences around.) The final stage, which showed the near future, had soon become history. All the devices they predicted had come to be.

Rather than update the final stage, the show was cancelled. The building was repurposed and transformed into America Sings. Even that fun show ran its course. Innovations was next; that is what it was the last time I visited. Now, I believe it is Star Wars Launch

Pad, whatever that is. I haven't been to Disneyland in quite a while. That's sad.

Anyway, the reason I rambled down that section of memory lane is to bring up the future. Progress continues to happen, and it is more than a carousel; it is a vortex of progress! (Perhaps toroid of progress is better?) We have been moving forward for a long time.

Living life is changing and growing in all aspects—growing into *what-ifs*. If you want to predict the future accurately, create it!

Four in One

The four I's are instinct, intellect, intuition, and intention—or body, mind, soul, and spirit. Everything may be segregated into these groups. Instinct/body is where the cash flow fits. It is the most visible, yet least important. *Interface* is a great I-word. It is the interface between each of the aspects that drives synergistic growth in the individual. I am I.

The past is what makes the present what it is. The future is where the present is going. You have control over both. History is done, yet it can be recreated. Seriously. Changing the past is possible. (Okay, to be fair, it is only the focus that changes, but that is what defines the past.) Changing focus to the future creates the desired results. Have a soft focus on the past and sharp focus on the future while living in the present. All is now.

In fact, while thinking of the future, I was reminded of the distant past—a dream of the history of the kingdom(s) of man, including future history. I'll just cut to the chase: Daniel tells Nebuchadnezzar his dream. It was Nebuchadnezzar's dream, but Daniel told him what it was and interpreted it for him.

Your majesty, while you were watching, you observed an enormous statue. This magnificent statue stood before you with extraordinary brilliance. Its appearance was terrifying.

That statue had a head made of pure gold, with its chest and arms made of silver, its abdomen and thighs made of bronze, its legs made of iron, and its feet made partly of iron and partly of clay.

As you were watching, a rock was quarried—but not with human hands—and it struck the iron and clay feet of the statue, breaking them to pieces.

Then the iron, the clay, the bronze, the silver, and the gold were broken in pieces together and became like chaff from a summer threshing floor that the breeze carries away without leaving a trace. Then the rock that struck the statue grew into a huge mountain and filled the entire earth.[5]

So, here we have a statue that embodies the entire system of the world, the whole history of the cabal and the powers that be since Nebuchadnezzar started it all. For now, we will just accept the fact that this statue of different metals is representative of all of the systems' rise to domination. There are plenty of studies that break down each section of the statue and connect it with history. (We are down in the clay/iron toes right now, for those who know this bit of eschatology, the last gasp of the Roman Empire.) It is an interesting study. Let's skip a bit to the wrap-up where Daniel is talking about the distant future and the leaders of the end times:

---

[5] Daniel 2:31–35 ISV

During the reigns of those kings, the God of heaven will set up a kingdom that will never be destroyed, nor its sovereignty left in the hands of another people. It will shatter and crush all of these kingdoms, and it will stand forever.

Now, just as you saw that the stone was cut out of the mountain without human hands—and that it crushed the iron, bronze, clay, silver, and gold to pieces—so also the great God has revealed to the king what will take place after this. Your dream will come true, and its meaning will prove trustworthy.[6]

A stone, not cut by human hands, strikes the base of the statue, destroying it. Then this stone grows into a mountain that covers the earth and beyond—the everlasting kingdom of God.

There is a movement going on behind the scenes—the transformation of the system of the world into what it is intended to be. I suggest that this movement is online and unstoppable. What the Tower of Babel attempted to accomplish will be accomplished in the Internet—intangible and cut without hands, cyberspace set in silicon chips.

Is an outside force a required catalyst for the ascension? Or can individual instigators catalyze and grow organically from grassroots movements? Who really built the Internet?

What are you doing to move into the new kingdom?

God Is Within

God with a big G and gods with a little g—it is curious how humans prefer to look outside of themselves, looking for someone to blame,

---

6 Daniel 2:44–45 ISV

shirking responsibility. Principalities and powers are the hierarchy we build to save us from ourselves. It is time to see the connection. We are all connected! Each a worthy piece of the All.

Time for *Introspection*!

Time is an illusion. That is what I thought. How is time perceived? Is what we call time simply the perceivable bit of the real dimension of time? It behooves us to take the time to find out.

What really happened at the Tower of Babel? Was humankind different before Elohim confused and scattered? Did we *physically* change?

The bicameral mind, did it exist pre-Tower of Babel? The corpus callosum, or tough body (of connection), bridges the gap between brain hemispheres. Did something happen to change this structure of the brain? Did we blind our *third eye* by minding the gap of the mind?

Instinct, intellect, intuition, and intention are the four aspects of you. Are you an equal aspect employer?

It is the perception of time which makes it seem pliable. I suppose this is why the Greeks had two words for time, Chronos and Kairos. Kairos is the word we in the west don't have an equivalent for. It is an interesting concept that there are two types of time. I think Chronos is linear and Kairos is cyclical. Tick and Tock. Two steps forward, one back. Tick is Chronos, Tock is Kairos. The music is reversible, but time is not... turn back! (Yay, ELO reference! Face the mighty waterfall!)

Manifest *the Secret*

Partly because it is no longer a secret, there is a cultish feel for it. It was the name-it-and-claim-it cults in the '70s and '80s.

These are all based on tapping into the source of all things and *extracting what you want*. You can call this source God, Allah, the Universe, Tao, *or whatever*. It is based on the connection we all have with the source code of the everything. *The law of one* fits right in with this phenomenon.

I didn't understand the DC Comic's Green Lantern character at all until I became aware of manifestation and the Secret. I thought it just silly that a ring would make anything the guy wanted. It was just wishing, in my mind. Then I realized the ring enhanced the latent powers of the user, like Dumbo's feather. (In the beloved film by Disney, Dumbo was given a *magic feather* by the crows to help him believe he could fly.) It was the scaffold used while building. Once the building is done, the scaffold should be removed.

Inquiring. What is the scaffold we can assemble when we individuate? What are the steps for cycling through individuation improvement? It may seem cyclical, but because of time, it is actually a vortex. Vortices are spiraling toward zero point, in fact, an eternal toroidal machine. Tap into that power.

Everything is a glimpse into *the Source*, the source of *the force*. The blind men and the elephant is a great, yet simple analogy. Each describes the elephant differently because he only feels a portion. In the land of the blind, the one-eyed man is king. Activation of the third eye is a step toward seeing. Keep in mind that even people with two good eyes don't always see.

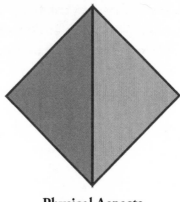

Physical Aspects

Let's look at instinct. Just because this is associated with body doesn't mean it is completely visible. In fact, most of what makes instinct is hidden. In the computer analogy, perhaps instinct is the firmware. It is the framework that all software must run in. We won't go as far as to say instinct is hardware because it can be overridden. It can be changed like a good BIOS. It is just as dangerous if not done properly. It is possible to break your instinct. Shattered minds are not easily repaired. Not even a full reboot will overcome some problems. PTSD may be irreparable in some cases.

Let's look at intellect. Here we associate with the mind. The brain is not the container of the mind; rather, it is the interface. In fact, the whole body contains the mind, and the mind extends beyond the body. The body is more of a local Internet. So much data is stored in this local Internet, and more is added moment by moment. Read *The Biology of Belief* by Bruce Lipton. Every cell in your body is a component of this local network. We can call it your innernet. It is your representation in this dimension/density. Firmware, software, and wetware all come together to manipulate the hardware. The hardware is your avatar on this plane. Oh, and the body/mind that makes you you is only part of your whole.

Instinct and intellect are the two aspects that make up the physical you. There is the spiritual you too. The spiritual you is made up of the two aspects intuition and intellect. You're made up of a two-two—the two-two of you. The tetrahedral intersection of these four aspects is the distortion field that makes you you. You are a distortion of the One.

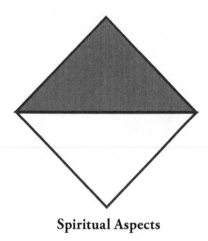

Spiritual Aspects

Let's look at intuition. Here, we associate with the soul, the unseen essence that is eternal and outside of the prison of time. The One is outside of time. You are a distortion of the One in time. Time is the fuel for the toroidal engine of life. Time is what makes learning possible. You are an aspect of the One's introspection, a subroutine of sorts. You are helping determine the question that results in 42. The soul is you pulling the strings on your meat puppet.

Let's look at intention. Whose line is it? The intent drives the engine of life. Here is where your responsibility originates. Intention is what you have planned. What happens happens because of your blueprint or intent. You may feel out of control because you've handed your project over to someone else, yet you are responsible for handing it over. Whatever you allow others to do with your life is determined by your allowance.

Good or bad, the outcome is fully your responsibility. If you give control away, you lose control. And just like losing control in a car, you will face the consequences. You will feel the impact. If you are in an automobile with self-driving capabilities, and it impacts something, you feel the impact.

Individuate—Intrastate or Interstate

What have we discussed so far? We move past the trilogy of body, mind, and spirit, adding another dimension: time. I have assigned one word to each of the aspects of our individuality to represent body, mind, soul, and spirit.

Instinct, Intellect, Intuition, and Intention

Remember the tetrahedron is the first Platonic solid, a shape with four sides. This shape represents the basic building block of our dimension. The photon is in this shape. Let there be light!

On the Hawaiian island of Oahu, there is a wonderful interstate highway. If that doesn't make you pause, you may not realize that an interstate highway is one that goes to *another* state. Technically, the term for the highway is intrastate, because it is contained within the state. (In fact, it doesn't even go to another island within the State of Hawaii.) Yes, I understand that it had to be called that to receive federal funding, and perhaps because it goes to a seaport and an airport, it may be considered interstate for commerce. But since those are both good I-words, let's apply them to the I. Let's call it *intrastate* when you are working within one of the four I's and *interstate* when you work with two or more of the four I's at the same time.

The One is I am that I am—infinite self-perception.

Change is growth. Curve is change. Everyone is different; that's the point! Everyone must change to grow.

Frog in the Kettle

The frog in the kettle analogy is usually used as a warning against change. As the story goes, because frogs are not warm-blooded, their body temperature is dependent on the ambient temperature. If you put them in a kettle of hot water, they will jump right out, but if you put them in a kettle and warm the water slowly, they will not notice and jump out when it gets too hot. They will simply perish in the frog stew.

The analogy is change can happen slowly, and you will tolerate and acclimate to it. If enough small disagreements occur over time, a large change can occur, eventually eliminating your original destiny and purpose.

How Aesop Ruined My Life!

The Greek historian Herodotus mentioned in passing that "Aesop the fable writer" was a slave who lived in Ancient Greece during the fifth century BCE. Do you realize how many stories are attributed to Aesop? Stories with morals, that is what they are. There are over six hundred of these fables said to originate from this slave/storyteller. That seems a bit much. But there is a lot of material to choose from. One that comes to mind is about the ant and grasshopper; this one had a big impact on me and my work ethic. I wonder how many of his fables truly impacted my life. This rumination of ruination is most intriguing.

The gist of my ruination is summed up in the race of the tortoise and the hare. Working to emulate the tortoise made me slow and methodical. Any speed increase I attributed to the hare, who was *not* to be emulated. Of course, it was my skewed interpretation that was the actual cause of my ruination.

Let's look at the story to refresh our minds.

> The hare was once boasting of his speed before the other animals. "I have never yet been beaten," said he, "when I put forth my full speed. I challenge anyone here to race with me."
>
> The tortoise said quietly, "I accept your challenge."
>
> "That is a good joke," said the hare. "I could dance 'round you all the way."
>
> "Keep your boasting till you've beaten me," answered the tortoise. "Shall we race?"
>
> So, a course was fixed, and a start was made. The hare darted almost out of sight at once but soon stopped and, to show his contempt for the tortoise, lay down to have a nap. The tortoise plodded on and plodded on, and when the hare awoke from his nap, he saw the tortoise just near the winning-post and could not run up in time to save the race. Then said the tortoise, "Plodding wins the race."

What does this story from Aesop have to do with anything? Well, slow and steady wins the race was a mantra. "It is who I am" is a meme planted deeply in me. It has steered my life. I am not happy about it.

I must point out that I cannot blame Aesop for my choices. I am responsible for everything I believe and do. In spin class, the saying was altered to "Strong and steady wins the race!" That works better for me now.

But we were talking about a frog in a kettle.

Feedback Loop

Continuous feedback of introspection and interaction (discussion) will help correct any drift—and correct an origin fallacy if needed. My argument has always been to constantly question everything in case you have been following a false premise.

Our daily use of GPS is a wonderful example.

The GPS constantly updates your known position in relation to your destination. The newer guidance systems will include data of current traffic and readjust to provide the quickest route. You can set the system up to avoid toll roads and freeways if you prefer. You can use the system to provide walking routes, public transportation routes, and so on. But in order for the system to work, you must be in constant contact with the satellites. If you don't have feedback from at least two of the satellites, there is no way of knowing where you are. The system will fail. Having more than two satellites provides better accuracy. Triangulation and error correction are constantly updated.

This is the same with your daily growth. If you are not connected, you are lost. If you are only connected to one source, you are lost. Connect through all four aspects that make you you.

Introspection *and* interaction are tools to begin with—and when we go through introspection, we must ask if we are looking at ourselves as we truly are or as we present ourselves? Growing up, my mother planted a deep meme by continuously repeating a quote: "Oh the gift that God would give us, to see ourselves as others see us!" Through her instilling this, I became aware that my looks, actions, words, and so on were all a reflection of who I am. People judge, so be careful. Here is the problem with that: it causes us to build a facade to show the world.

We all wear masks. Looking in a mirror only shows the mask.

So, decades of putting together this brick facade (all in all, just another brick) have made us "whitewashed sepulchers" as Jesus put it, nice and pretty on the outside but dead and rotting on the inside.

It is well said that we must begin by dealing with "the man in the mirror." But again, we must make sure we are not looking at a reflection of our facade; we need to get behind the curtain.

The Land of Oz

How can we see behind the curtain?

True introspection must get behind the facade. We need Toto to pull back the curtain. Yes, introspection must be done by the individual, but sometimes we need a little help to know where the curtain is; the rest of life distracts big league! We truly must find a way to get behind the scenes. Who is your Toto?

Pay attention to the man behind the curtain—that charlatan!

Funny, mentioning this analogy from Oz, I realized the four aspects of an individual are reflected in *The Wizard of Oz* by the four Yellow Brick Road sojourners:

Instinct—Cowardly Lion (courage)

Intellect—Scarecrow (brain)

Intuition—Tinman (heart)

Intention—Dorothy (home)

These four needed to work together with the man behind the curtain to find what they were missing. They needed some outside help to know he was there.

It is okay to ask the wizard for help; just remember to find the real person behind the curtain. Each view of yourself is just a portion of the integrated whole; you have all four aspects. Know and work on each one!

Individuating Integration— Action Plan

Individuation is a word coined by Carl Jung to refer to the process of growing as an individual—escaping from the automaton's single view life, breaking through the layers of crap piled on you from before you were conscious and self-aware. Family, friends, and society stunt the natural blossoming of your individuality. Your individuality is unique and intended to grow separate from everything else. It is all about experiencing life from a different point of view. Move past those Freudian slips once you understand where they come from. The filter between your subconscious and your conscious is clogged and bypassed. Years of skipping maintenance have taken their toll. It is time for an overhaul! To analyze the problems, a good technician will take a look at how the operation is occurring now and then compare it to how the operation *should* be occurring. I learned a long time ago, the first thing to do is determine what the machine is supposed to be doing. Only then can a systematic approach to finding the problem be formulated. "Garbage in; garbage out" is a saying to remind the technician to verify the inputs are as they should be.

Let's define individuation for this book first with a definition derived from dictionary.com:

individuation

in-duh-vij-oo-ey-shuh n

noun

> The act of individuating. State of being individuated; individual existence; individuality. Philosophy; the determination or contraction of a general nature to an individual mode of existence; development of the individual from the general.

Now, as Carl Jung established the meaning,

> Individuation is the process in which the individual self develops out of an undifferentiated unconscious—seen as a developmental psychic process during which innate elements of personality, the components of the immature psyche, and the experiences of the person's life become, if the process is more or less successful, integrated over time into a well-functioning whole.

Or as I like to say, individuation is the process of troubleshooting your life. It is best to learn how to do this on your own, because you are unique. Maintaining yourself is a very sensitive matter. There are times when you just don't have the tools or time to do the maintenance yourself, so you must get help. Even when you seek help from others, you must know what you need.

Troubleshooting

When I was troubleshooting an electronic cryptographic machine, I could go crazy replacing parts only to have the same problem occur. So, the first thing I would do would be to take the machine offline and put a known signal into it. I would verify that signal was at the first step of the process because it could be the connector the signal was coming in through that was defective.

It is the same thing with your car. A car is a complicated machine. Sure, they all have the same basic fit, form, and function, but each model is different. Even cars of the same model are different in some ways. How they are driven and maintained can be vastly different. One car could have 200,000 miles on the odometer while the other only has 80,000 miles. Of course, the one with the lower miles could be in worse shape if it has been driven hard and not maintained. As the saying goes, it's the years, not the mileage.

I Trouble

Let me tell you how I am addressing my I problem. (I used to call in sick and say I had an eye problem; I just couldn't see going in to work!)

I suggest you get a notebook with at least four tabs in it. This book is for "your I's only." You will collect information and track successes. This book is going to be your own copy of the *Individual User's Guide: A Manual for an I Exam.*

You've got to reflect and connect.

The I's are the windows to the sole! (See, there is a play on *two* words there!) Be the sole survivor! Be the soul survivor! You can give your soul away, you can sell your soul, or you can keep your soul. It is the pearl of great price! It is worth selling everything to get it. "What does it profit a man to gain the whole world but lose his soul?"[7]. Do you have a sole purpose, a soul purpose, or a sold purpose?

---

[7] Mark 8:36

On the bottom of your shoe, you have a sole. It is for walking on. It protects you from the harsh road. Is there a good word-play analogy there? I think so. Sole can mean single, and sole can be the bottom of a shoe. It's best not to confuse the two; you will get walked on.

Your Manual and Your Books

What's on your bookshelf? You are what you read! Do you ever read? How do you keep track of where you are in life? Do you read science fiction or science faction? (*Faction* is a word that means a subset of a larger group.)

Mind Tripping

Let's go on a mind trip, a thought experiment. Imagine the truth of the universe is that whatever you think is true. No, really, just like Green Lantern, you can manifest anything needed. Now imagine that the universe adapts to grant every thought, but the thoughts of two individuals can cancel each other out. There is a safety valve on the universe that keeps things from heating up.

Conway's Game of Life

We used to play this on graph paper.

Life is an infinite two-dimensional orthogonal grid of square cells, each of which is in one of two possible states, "populated" or "unpopulated." Every cell interacts with its eight neighbors, which are the cells that are horizontally, vertically, or diagonally adjacent. At each step in time, the following transitions occur:

- Any live cell with fewer than two live neighbors dies of loneliness.

- Any live cell with two or three live neighbors lives on to the next generation.
- Any live cell with more than three live neighbors dies of overcrowding.
- Any dead cell with exactly three live neighbors becomes a live cell, as if by reproduction.

The initial pattern constitutes the seed of the system. The first generation is created by applying these rules simultaneously to every cell in the seed—births and deaths occur simultaneously, and the discrete moment at which this happens is sometimes called a tick (in other words, each generation is a pure function of the preceding one). The rules continue to be applied repeatedly to create further generations.

Does that make sense?

What would happen if you started the whole board with all occupied squares? Everyone would die of overpopulation. If you started with all empty squares, it would never have a chance for life. But if you start with some squares occupied and some empty, you could see life and death each pass. The idea is the starting tick provides the action for the rest of time. (So, God would have to separate the light from the dark, eh?)

Some people think this is what happened when God started the universe. He made all the rules, set all the pieces in place, and let it go. The universe is continuing with no interaction from God. He is just observing.

Time to Go!

Let's use the Chinese game of Go as analogy of light verses dark. There are two types of marbles, black and white. There is a grid. Each player can place his or her marbles on the board, one at a time. There are fixed rules to this game. No two games are ever exactly alike. It is a strategy game. (You can use a Go board to play Conway's game of life too.)

The Rules of Go

A game of Go starts with an empty board. Each player has an effectively unlimited supply of pieces (called stones), one taking the black stones, the other taking white. The main objective of the game is to use your stones to form territories by surrounding vacant areas of the board. It is also possible to capture your opponent's stones by completely surrounding them.

Players take turns, placing one of their stones on a vacant point at each turn, with black playing first. Note that stones are placed on the intersections of the lines rather than in the squares, and once played, stones are not moved. However, they may be captured, in which case they are removed from the board and kept by the capturing player as prisoners.

At the end of the game, the players count one point for each vacant point inside their own territory and one point for every stone they have captured. The player with the larger total of territory plus prisoners is the winner.

Conway's game of life is known as a zero-player game. That is interesting; yet it still requires an outside source to initiate. It is easier to find an electronic version online than to play with graph paper like the "good ol' days."

Back to Individuation

We were talking about individuation and finding tools to help an individual become more so. The integration of the four I's is key—balance and control, just like riding a bike. Actually, a bicycle is a good metaphor. We have two wheels, physical and metaphysical. Think of a bicycle with two spheres as wheels. Each sphere is two sections, like a baseball skin—sacred geometry at work here. On a sphere, a triangle can have angles that add up to more than 180 degrees. Hmmm, that just reminded me of how waves out of phase by 180 degrees cancel each other out. Triangles are the only polygon with angles that add up to 180 degrees. We can perhaps draw some information from that. Anything with four or more angles has twice the total at 360 degrees, all the way up to a circle, which has infinite angles.

Maintenance of I is not something that should be debated. It is something you should never push off onto someone else to do for you. There is nobody who can know you as well as you can. I know there are people who seem to know me better than I know myself, but realistically, it is an outside view and usually only of one or two facets. Going deeper in yourself is the only way to know yourself. Commit to understanding the only individual in existence you are responsible for. Look deep into your own I's. The I's have it!

Write your own user's guide! One goal for this book to help people understand they weren't born with a user's guide tucked under their pillow. A journal is a great way to document what you discover. Sharing what you have found out about yourself with loved ones may encourage them to grow too. One thing you must always remember is that what works for you may not work for someone else. You may find a yogurt that does wonders for you, but your friend may be lactose intolerant, and it would do damage rather than good.

How to Write Your Own User's Guide to Life

You are the only one who can. You need to collaborate with others to zero in on what you need. You need to list the tools and fix-it shops available to you for the times you can't fix it yourself. You need to pay attention to the help you do get and make sure it fits you. You may find the tool you have to fix a certain problem will only work once. Sometimes the repair will change the way you work. Sometimes the fix-it shop fixes the symptom but the problem simmers below the surface. That is why you must always pay attention. Know what those check engine lights on the dashboard mean. There is more than one problem that can make that appear.

Switch Hitting

It also brings to mind the first time I switched to playing racquetball with my left hand. It was comical, and the first game was really tough. But I started to get used to it. What was amazing was how the world appeared different when I walked out of the court. Everything just looked different. Here is a challenge, write every day with your nondominant hand. You don't need to share it with anyone, just spend a half hour every day for a month writing with your other hand. It will be comical at first. You will be amazed at how much you improve over the month. Plus, you will discover and see things you've never seen before. Switching things up is important in life. Our body is designed (or evolved) to conserve energy. It will improve the muscles needed for a task you do frequently so you can learn to minimize the cost of doing it. Continuous improvement is part of the design (or evolutionary accident).

This book is a discovery of self. It is not a book of regimented actions for you to take to be like me. Don't be like me. I am writing it because I would like to have had a book like this during my struggle. I could call the book *My Struggle*, but that is too close to the title Adolph Hitler used for his book. My book is not how following me will make you and the nation stronger. It is, however, a book to encourage you to make you and your nation—and the world—stronger.

Stay Mindful

Keeping aware of advancements and trends is a crucial part of your I care. The coming singularity is frightening many people. I suggest a good reading of *The Diamond Age* and several other books by Neal Stephenson. Technology is scary magic to those who don't understand it. We are moving into a golden age, not the postapocalyptic nightmare most people are expecting. (Oh, that brings me back to the idea that we are cocreating the world as we go; if enough people push for that scenario, it may happen! Stop doing that!) By knowing what is coming, you can manifest to be a part of the change. Ride the wave, or get pummeled by it!

The first and every next step in individuation is to take action. A plan without action isn't a plan at all. Unless steps are implemented, nothing happens. The road to hell is paved with good intentions. Let's not make the road to hell the easy road to travel on. That should be the rough and unpassable road. Two roads diverged in the forest, and I took the road less traveled on. Wide is the road that leads to destruction; narrow is the path that leads to righteousness. Remember, an object at rest cannot be stopped. It also tends to stay at rest. It takes much more energy to move an object at rest than to divert the course of one already in motion.

I suppose intention requires action. Intention is the second data point required with GPS—the destination. Intention is setting the destination. If you don't know where you are going, any road will take you there. Not a very efficient way to travel. If you know your destination and where you are currently, it is a simple matter of mapping out route options and choosing one. Start and finish are the only two pieces of info needed. (Well, it is important to have an accurate map.) Assuming the GPS has the map, the starting point, and the destination, it is only a matter of progressing forward, the continuous feedback of your current location and objects in your way, traffic patterns, and so on. It is only a matter of time until you reach the goal. Recalculating—yes, you will get there.

If you start with bad intent, you may find the way difficult. Perhaps the universe will fight against you. Perhaps the intention of others will cancel you out. Service-to-self people are working with bad intention (bad intention toward others but good intention for self).

The Basics

The four I's are instinct, intellect, intuition, and intention. These four are interconnected with one another. Instinct is surrounded by intellect, intuition, and intention. Intellect is surrounded by instinct, intuition, and intention. Intuition is surrounded by instinct, intellect, and intention. Intention is surrounded by instinct, intellect, and intuition. If we apply a color to each I, the triangles representing each one will have an edge of each of the other colors. That may be illustrative too. Let me see if I remember the colors I applied. Red is instinct. Blue is intellect. Yellow is intuition. White is intention. Those feel right to me. But use whatever works best for your visualization.

Once again, intention is the focus on the goal. The shortest distance between two points is a straight line.

Keep Moving

It is not the destination; it is the journey. The destination is the One Source. That sounds contradictory. It is like saying, "Yes, Lord, *but!*" If He is Lord, how can you disagree? Well, I believe free will is all about that. You are allowed to disagree with God. Running down the list of people you mustn't piss off, I would suspect the Creator of everything might be at the top of the list.

Collective Intention

When JFK set the US intention on safely landing a man on the moon and returning him safely, it was nigh impossible. But the nation rallied together and made it happen. The impossible became possible. Not only did we accomplish that, but there was a big list of products that were invented for the project and became ubiquitous. Did you know the cell phone you have in your hand has more computing power than the entire computing network used to land a man on the moon?

Synergy only happens when free individuals come together under a common intention. Stay free, and work willingly with others—not because it is easy, but because it is hard!

Write on!

Remember the power of the written word. Journal because your I matters!

> All scripture is given by inspiration of God, and is profitable for doctrine, for reproof, for correction, for instruction in righteousness:
>
> That the man of God may be perfect, thoroughly furnished unto all good works[8].

Create your own "living and active" scriptures as you discover I.

> For the word of God is alive and active. Sharper than any double-edged sword, it penetrates even

---

[8] 2 Timothy 3:16-17 King James Version (KJV)

to dividing soul and spirit, joints and marrow; it judges the thoughts and attitudes of the heart[9].

Join other manifestations of the One Source at FourViewsOfI.com in collective individual discovery.

---

[9] Hebrews 4:12 New International Version (NIV)

I-Word Index

The *I*'s have it! I have been partial to words that begin with the letter I, including: instinct, intellect, intuition, and intention. For your amusement and introspection, here are select words found in this book which begin with I.

About the Author

Stephen Rousseau, AKA Stever, is back at ground zero in belief. Not disgruntled... just wary. He intends to encourage everyone to QUESTION EVERYTHING and to THINK ABOUT IT! Know that you are responsible for only one person, YOURSELF!

After his long life on the treadmill as a manufacturing engineer, test engineer, project manager, etc. ended unexpectedly when sacrificially fired, he jumped into life. A lifelong fascination with storytelling, particularly through multi-media - movies, television, etc. is leading this desire to help people streamline workflow as well as find the value in each step they take.

Helping others discover their individuality and worth by sharing what he has learned along the way, helping others avoid pitfalls of life.

Let's all help each other grow abundantly.